QUALITATIVE RESEARCH:
INTELLIGENCE FOR COLLEGE STUDENTS

Wayne L. Davis, Ph.D.
&
Ann-Marie C. Buchanan, Ph.D.

BALBOA
PRESS

A DIVISION OF HAY HOUSE

Balboa Press books may be ordered through booksellers or by contacting:

Balboa Press
A Division of Hay House
1663 Liberty Drive
Bloomington, IN 47403
www.balboapress.com
1 (877) 407-4847

Because of the dynamic nature of the Internet, any web addresses or links contained in this book may have changed since publication and may no longer be valid. The views expressed in this work are solely those of the author and do not necessarily reflect the views of the publisher, and the publisher hereby disclaims any responsibility for them.

The author of this book does not dispense medical advice or prescribe the use of any technique as a form of treatment for physical, emotional, or medical problems without the advice of a physician, either directly or indirectly. The intent of the author is only to offer information of a general nature to help you in your quest for emotional and spiritual well-being. In the event you use any of the information in this book for yourself, which is your constitutional right, the author and the publisher assume no responsibility for your actions.

Any people depicted in stock imagery provided by Thinkstock are models, and such images are being used for illustrative purposes only.
Certain stock imagery © Thinkstock.

Print information available on the last page.

ISBN: 978-1-5043-4823-2 (sc)
ISBN: 978-1-5043-4825-6 (hc)
ISBN: 978-1-5043-4824-9 (e)

Library of Congress Control Number: 2016902364

Balboa Press rev. date: 3/11/2016

PREFACE

Reading about a problem may be good (a literature review), but learning how to investigate the problem yourself is better. Research is a systematic process of collecting, analyzing, and interpreting information in order to better understand the subject of study. All research involves theory, collects some type of data, and attempts to solve a problem by answering a question. A quantitative research study indicates how variables are numerically related and may be used to determine the method of operandi and to make predictions based on confidence levels. A qualitative study indicates why variables are related and may be used to determine motives. In either case, by manipulating the independent variables, the dependent variables may be effectively managed. This book is written for college students and focuses on qualitative research. A comprehensive qualitative research study is presented within this book.

PART I

Table of Contents

List of Tables

List of Figures

CHAPTER 1. ACADEMIC RESEARCH

Why conduct academic research?

Academic research has the highest level of credibility. Academic research involves theory and the collection and analysis of data in order to solve a problem (Balian, 1988). Academic research involves processes that enhance the validity and reliability of the data and findings. Academic publications in peer-reviewed, scholarly sources require the work to be critiqued and approved by experts in the field. See Table 1 for an analogy between choice of police weapon and level of credibility.

Table 1

Analogy between Choice of Police Weapon and Type of Reference

Strength of Resource	Police Weapon for Deadly Force Encounter	Level of Credibility for Argument
Strong	Gun	Scholarly, Peer-reviewed, Academic Research Article
Moderate	Baton	Textbook/Magazine Article
Weak	Fists	Personal Opinion

Research

Research is a systematic process of collecting, analyzing, and interpreting information in order to better understand the subject of study (Balian, 1988). Research attempts to solve a problem by answering a question. A qualitative research study indicates **why** variables are related, based on feelings, opinions, and perceptions. This is especially important if the motive for a particular behavior needs to be investigated. A quantitative research study, on the other hand, indicates **how** variables are numerically related and is especially important if the method of operandi for a particular event needs to be investigated. Quantitative research allows predictions to be made based on confidence levels. Qualitative and quantitative studies have equal value; each type of study only provides half of the information. In other words, neither one is necessarily better than the other. Although it may be time and cost prohibitive in many cases, a mixed study may be conducted. A mixed study is a study that utilizes both qualitative and quantitative research techniques, which provides more comprehensive information. See Figure 1 (Lutterman, 2015).

It should be noted that both qualitative and quantitative research studies have independent and dependent variables. By understanding **how** and **why** variables are related, people in authority may be able to manipulate the independent variables in order to manage the dependent variable. By manipulating the independent variables (e.g., perception of crime, perception of the police, sport participation, etc.), the dependent variables (e.g., riots, child abuse, aggression, etc.) may be effectively managed. For example, if the number of training hours is inversely related to the number of complaints received against police officers (quantitative study), then a police department may require more training hours for its officers. On the other hand, if residents engage in riots because they feel that the police are abusive (qualitative study), then the residents' feelings will need to be better understood and addressed. See Table 2 for the differences between qualitative and quantitative research.

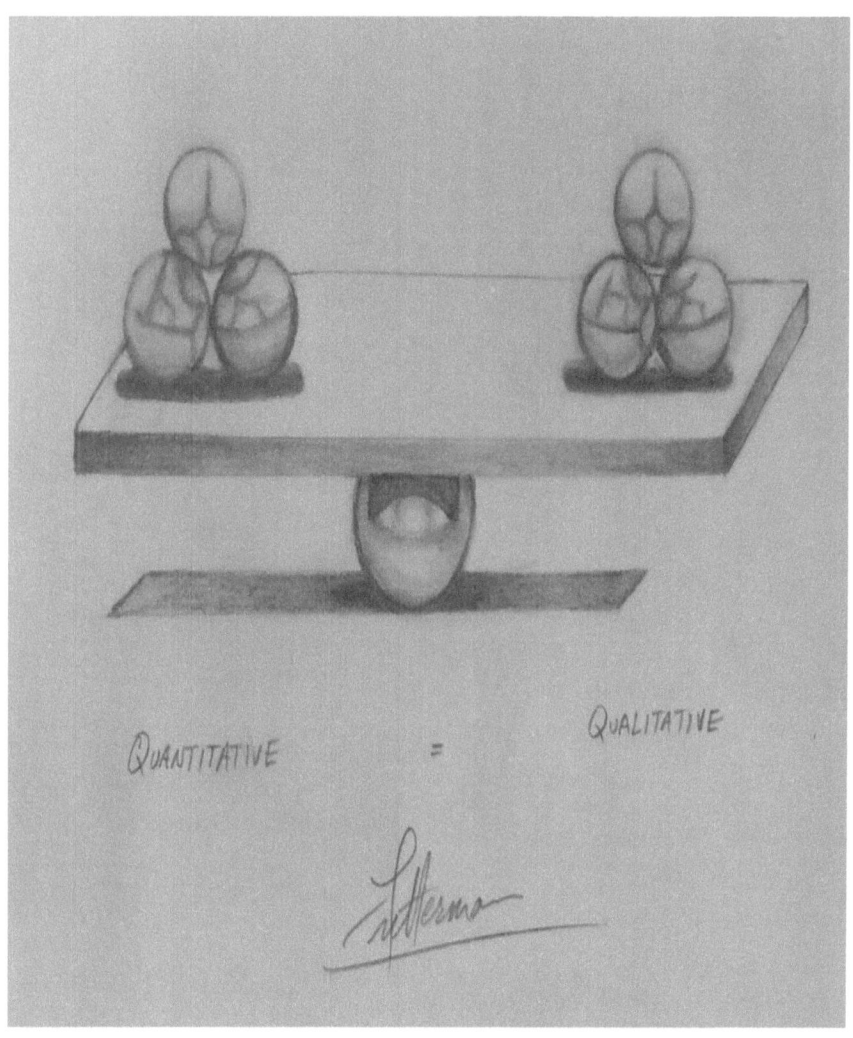

QUANTITATIVE = QUALITATIVE

Figure 1. Comprehensive Information Requires Both Qualitative and Quantitative Data.

Table 2

Differences between Qualitative and Quantitative Research (Leedy & Ormrod, 2016)

	Qualitative	Quantitative
Purpose	To explore; To describe; To explain why variables are related; To develop a theory	To predict; To confirm; To explain how variables are related; To validate
Perspective	Believes the subjective experience of the insider provides the most meaningful data	Objectively tries to understand the facts from an outside perspective
Research Process	Personal perspectives; Unknown variables; Flexible guidelines	Focused; Known variables; Preplanned methods
Data Format	Textual; Images; Informal; Reality changes; Small sample	Numerical; Standardized instruments; Facts do not change; Large sample
Data Analysis	Themes; Categories; Subjective; Inductive reasoning; Allows all naturally occurring variables to influence results	Statistics; Objective; Deductive reasoning; Attempts to control extraneous variables
Findings	Words; Narratives; Personal	Numbers; Formal
Research Questions	Research Questions; Probe Questions	Research Questions; Null Hypotheses

Examples of Questions (RQ = Research Question; PQ = Probe Question; HO = Null Hypothesis)	RQ: How do you perceive being spanked as a child by your father has influenced your attitude toward your spouse? PB1: Do you believe that your father was a fair man when you were a child? PB2: Do you feel that your father loved you when he was spanking you? PB3: Do you feel that your father had a favorite child?	RQ1: Is there a relationship between the amount of religiosity and the crime rate? HO1: There is no relationship between the amount of religiosity and the crime rate? RQ2: Is there a relationship between the number of times being spanked as a child and level of aggression? HO2: There is no relationship between the number of times being spanked as a child and level of aggression?

Wayne L. Davis, Ph.D. & Ann-Marie C. Buchanan, Ph.D.

Quantitative Research

Quantitative investigations are scientific, objective, and effective in describing phenomena in terms of magnitude (Balian, 1988). Quantitative investigations use numeric values and statistics to identify patterns, to objectively quantify relationships between variables, and to make predictions. In addition, because large sample sizes are used, data can be generalized to larger populations. However, numeric values are ineffective in describing the subjective interpretations of human emotions (Wakefield, 1995). Because individuals have unique lived experiences and their realities are based on their own perceptions, a single objective truth is unattainable; indeed, there are multiple realities when dealing with perceptions. Thus, quantitative investigations are ineffective for the reconstruction of meanings. In short, quantitative studies ask **how** variables are related but not **why** they are related. For example, a quantitative research question may ask, *Is there a relationship between ice cream sales and the murder rate?* In fact, there is a relationship, but trying to solve the murder rate by outlawing the sale of ice cream will be ineffective because the sale of ice cream does not cause murder (Davis, 2015). Failing to properly identify the root cause of the problem will result in a waste of resources.

If you conducted a qualitative study and asked people **why** they commit murder when ice cream sales are high, perhaps they will tell you that they commit murder when it is hot (ice cream sales to them may be irrelevant). When it is hot, perhaps the heat agitates them to a point of violence, they may be more mobile (compared to when there are snow covered roads in the winter), and they may have more targets available to them in public.

Types of Research

There are many different types of academic research. The appropriate research design will depend on the purpose and focus of the study. See Table 3 for various types of research.

Table 3

Type of Research and its Purpose (Leedy & Ormrod, 2016)

Type of Research	Purpose
Action Research	To find a solution to a local problem in a local setting
Case Study	To learn about a poorly understood problem from a single person
Ethnography	To study a cultural group in a natural setting
Grounded Theory	To derive a theory by collecting and analyzing data over various stages
Phenomenological Research	To understand the participants' point-of-view about a topic
Observation Study	To objectively and systematically assess actions via observations
Developmental Research	To observe and describe data via a cross-sectional or longitudinal study
Content Analysis	To identify patterns, biases, or themes in the data
Historic Research	To reconstruct and interpret historical events
Ex Post Facto Research	To look at past events to predict current events
Experimental Research	To measure the consequences of research-imposed treatments of randomly selected participants
Quasi-experimental Research	To measure the consequences of research-imposed treatments of non-randomly selected participants
Survey Research	To collect a large amount of data, in a short amount of time, in a uniform manner
Correlational Research	To determine the quantitative relationships between two or more variables
Weibull Distribution	Test-to-failure analysis; continuous probability distribution. Predicts how long a product will survive at a given confidence level. Good for very low volume, such as with prototypes.

Theories

As stated earlier, **all research involves theory**, collects some type of data, and attempts to solve a problem by answering a question. Theories help explain problems, they provide possible solutions to the problems, and they guide the questions that are to be asked on a survey when collecting data (for validity). For example, if the social learning theory is being used to explain a problem (i.e., learning because of the frequency, intensity, duration, and importance of social learning experiences), it does not make sense to ask biological-based questions on a survey (i.e., diet, medications, etc.). In other words, if the social learning theory is being used to explain the problem, then the social learning theory must be used to solve the problem.

Assumptions

All theories rely on assumptions, which may impact the effectiveness of any decisions based on those theories. Understanding theories is important because applying the wrong theory to solve a problem will be less than optimal. This is why Megan's Law is proving to be less than effective. According to research on Megan's Law, the deterrence theory and labeling theory are being used to solve a biological-based problem (Corrigan, 2006). Thus, the proposed solution is not in alignment with the theories used to explain the problem and, consequently, Megan's Law is less than effective.

Decisions depend on assumptions, and we will never know if all of the assumptions are 100% accurate. Although we may be confident about a decision, we cannot know with absolute certainty that the decision is correct. However, understanding the assumptions that were relied upon in making a decision is important because the assumptions may change, which may impact best-practice decisions.

Table 4

Various Criminal Theories and their Limitations (Fay, 1987; Schmalleger, 2011; Sower, & Gist, 1994; Sower, Holland, Tiedke, & Freeman, 1957; Turvey & Petherick, 2009)

Theory	Description	Critique
Rational Choice Theory / Deterrence Theory	People freely choose their behaviors. Individuals evaluate the benefits versus costs ratio for each potential course of action. If the benefits are greater than costs, then the decision to perform that act is favorable. Rational choice theory focuses on benefits and on all costs. Deterrence theory focuses on legal costs. The deterrence theory relies on three factors: celerity, severity, and certainty of punishment.	Overemphasizes importance of individual choice; social factors, such as poverty, are dismissed; does not adequately consider emotions; target hardening causes displacement of crime; factors of deterrence may promote crime if all three factors are not effectively implemented simultaneously (certainty, severity, and celerity of punishment)
Routine Activities Theory	Crime occurs when three elements converge: motivated offenders, attractive targets, and the absence of capable guardians.	Level of motivation is not well defined; attractive targets and the absence of capable guardians are emphasized more than the motivated offender.
Durkheim's Mechanical Community	Social order and solidarity depend on the residents' reliance on each other to perform their specified tasks; interdependence is required.	Mechanical communities are isolated from other groups, and law enforcement promotes the uniformity of social norms in the local area; outsiders will be considered deviant.
Neoclassical Theory	Being tough on crime and retribution will curtail future crime.	Does not explain why crime decreases in areas without tough on crime policies; crime rate reductions may be due to demographic changes in the population.

Biological Theory	Human beings are biological creatures who are born with certain hardware, such as a brain, that controls thought and behavioral development. Because the brain uses a complex chemical-electrical process during the processing of information, any impairment in this process may interfere with the effective operation of the brain. Body shape, diet, hormones, environmental pollution, and chemical factors cause crime.	Denies role of free will; not everyone who is exposed to the same chemicals behave in the same way. Why is there no specific diet to cure crime? Increased exposure to pollution has not increased the crime rate; cannot explain crime in different parts of the country.
Sociobiology Theory	Behaviors are embedded in the process of natural selection and human survival; crime is the result of territorial struggles.	Fails to consider culture, social learning, and personal experiences; equates humans to animals.
Psychoanalytic Perspective Theory	Crime is the result of poorly developed superegos.	Lacks scientific support; elements of the theory were not applied to a wide context for society as a whole.
Social Learning Theory / Modeling Theory / Differential Association Theory	Criminal behaviors are learned through communications with intimate others; definitions favorable to crime exceed definitions unfavorable to crime; individuals learn behaviors by observing how others are rewarded and punished; frequency, duration, intensity, and importance of social learning experiences impact the learning of behaviors.	Pro-social and anti-social behaviors are simultaneously-learned through the same cognitive and behavioral mechanisms; does not consider free choice; does not explain why those surrounded by crime do not commit crime; only accounts for the communication of criminal values, not the emergence of criminal values.
Behavior Theory	The surrounding environment impacts behavior.	Dismisses cognition in human behavior; punishments may not deter martyrs; some groups believe that punishments are status-enhancing.
Theory of Collective Efficacy	The crime rate is increased due to the lack of individual resources, the lack of social knowledge, the lack of a stable family unit, the lack of	Influence of the theory varies by crime type and does not address the number of years that the effects will last; paramilitary gangs located in economically

	community participation, and the lack of juvenile supervision.	disadvantaged neighborhoods deliver important economic and social resources that promote informal social control.
Looking Glass Theory	People see themselves as others see them; people develop their individual identities by evaluating how they think that they appear to others, how they perceive that others judge their appearance, and by how others react to those judgments.	How an individual appears to other people is subjective because the appearance relies on interpretations and assumptions.
Strain Theory	Crime is the result of frustration due to blocked opportunities, which prevent success.	The U.S. provides opportunities for all Americans to financially succeed; claims that wealth is the single most important goal in life; delinquent juveniles do not report being more stressed than law abiding juveniles; does not adequately explain the lack of crime for women, who may be stressed as a result of continual discrimination.
Conflict Theory	People in power pass laws to protect their own self-interests. There is a struggle for power and laws are passed that penalize the disadvantaged.	Can be tautological and may lack explanatory power; may be racist because minorities (who have little power) are labeled as criminals; overstresses social change and dismisses other well-developed theories of crime; fails to recognize that most people believe crime should be controlled.
Containment Theory	Crime results when internal (e.g., positive self-esteem) and external (e.g., social groups) control mechanisms fail to protect the individual.	May be feelings of the moment that have been conditioned through individual thought mechanisms; only some people who are exposed to social pressures commit crime.

Hirschi's Social Bond Theory	People commit delinquent acts when their bonds to society are weak; the four bonds in Hirschi's theory involve attachment, commitment, involvement, and beliefs.	Individuals commit crime even when they know that it is wrong; social bonds do not appear strong enough to negate criminal behavior.
Interactional Theory	Crime is the result of a weakened bond between an individual and society combined with the learning of anti-social behaviors that are rewarded.	Does not fully appreciate childhood maltreatment, which leads to crime.
Social Control Theory	Delinquent behavior occurs when social constraints on antisocial behaviors are weakened. Control ratio predicts criminal behavior; Control ratio = amount of control personally experienced versus amount of control exercised over others. Too much or too little self-control are equally dangerous.	Assumes that all individuals are automatically deviant unless socialized through control mechanisms; dismisses learned behaviors and human motivations.
Self-control Theory	Crime is the result of the lack of individual self-control; children who are ineffectually parented before the age of eight develop less self-control than children of approximately the same age who are raised with better parenting skills; individuals have low self-esteem and seek immediate gratification; individuals have little patience and are frustrated easily.	Dismisses external factors during different stages of life; oversimplifies the causes of crime; does not define self-control and the tendency toward criminal behavior separately; suggests that the concepts of low self-control and the propensity for criminal behavior are one and the same.
Social Disorganization / Zone Theory	Crime associated with urban transition zones; crime is higher in low income zones near city; crime is linked to high transition areas where people have anonymity.	Too much credence to spatial location; does not apply to all types of crime, just street crime at the neighborhood level; does not explain organized crime, corporate crime, or deviant behavior that takes place outside neighborhood settings.

Labeling Theory	If individuals are arrested, this may result in a negative stigma being attached to them. This may consequently disrupt their personal relationships and may block their future legitimate economic opportunities, which may lead to additional crime.	Does not explain the origin of crime; does not explain secret deviants.
Broken Window Theory	Broken windows, graffiti, litter, public drinking, and abandoned vehicles indicate disorder and a lack of caring. If people do not care about their neighborhood, then this attracts crime.	May be artifact of police decision-making practices; may bear little objective relationship to the actual degree of crime in the area; police may focus more efforts in poor areas. For example, if the department patrols a certain area with more officers, the police should make more arrests in that area. Does a higher arrest rate mean safer streets or more dangerous streets?
Normative Sponsorship Theory	Indicates that people who have a convergence of interest may cooperate with one another in order to satisfy their needs	Community members will only work together as long as the goals are within the normal limits of established standards
Critical Social Theory	Practical social science that encourages individuals to become socially and politically active in order to change and improve their current social conditions; endorses the enlightenment, empowerment, and emancipation of the people: people are enlightened when they obtain empirical knowledge about their states of oppression and their potential capacity to improve their situations, people are empowered when they are galvanized to engage in a socially transformation action, people are emancipated when they know who they are, what they genuinely want, and when they have collective autonomy	Must raise the people's awareness of their current oppression; must demonstrate the possibility of a qualitatively different future; must hold community members responsible for actively getting involved and creating their own liberation.

	and power to freely and rationally determine the nature and course of their collective existence.	
Victim Precipitation	Victims unconsciously exhibit behaviors or characteristics that instigate or encourage the attackers; explains multiple victimizations	Relevant only to violent crimes or to particular forms of unlawful violence; assumes that victims and offenders interact prior to crime occurring.
Convict Criminology	Prisons are too big, hold too many people, and do not reduce crime; to control crime upon release from prison, prisons should focus more on treatment and less on security; based on the lived experiences of convicted felons and ex-inmates.	Most of the authors of the theory are white males, but not all are ex-convicts; authors are biased with agendas; non-convict feminists have been adding to the field, moving the theory from its roots.
Situational Crime Prevention (SCP) / Crime Prevention Through Environmental Design (CPTED)	SCP is a crime prevention strategy that attempts to eliminate or reduce the opportunities to commit specific crimes in specific locations by making crime more risky to attempt and more difficult to accomplish. Instead of relying upon law enforcers, the SCP strategy depends on public and private organizations. Furthermore, SCP and CPTED do not focus on the persons committing the crimes or the underlying causes of crime, such as unjust social and economic conditions, but focus instead on the settings for crime.	Only protects a limited geographical area; crime may be displaced.
Life Course Theory	Human lives are embedded in social relationships across the life span; the impact of various experiences depend on when they occur in life; each person makes choices, which impact each person's life course; a life course is shaped by historic times and places.	Many important life course determinants are experienced during childhood, which means adults may not be accountable for their crimes; individuals may select components of their life course and may influence their own trajectories.

Dual Taxonomic Theory	There are two types of offenders: life course persistent offenders (due to family dysfunction, poverty, neurophysiological deficits, and failure in school) and adolescence limited offenders (due to structural disadvantages).	Most antisocial children do not become criminals; family and psychological dysfunctions are not shown to be directly correlated to parent control or individual trajectories.
Developmental Pathways / Delinquent Development Theory	Anti-social behaviors are age dependent; as children age, they develop verbal coping skills, which help them manage conflict. Persistence in crime is influenced by many risk factors, such as broken homes, low family income, and harsh discipline. Desistance in crime has four factors: deceleration, specialization, de-escalation, and reaching a ceiling (plateau).	Aging causing desistance is meaningless because the theory fails to explain why desistance occurs; fails to explain free choice in human development.
Age-graded Theory	There is a positive relationship between social capital and pro-social behaviors; positive relationships are developed over time and lead to pro-social behaviors and reduced crime.	Positive relationships are subjective; some positive relationships may provide greater opportunities to commit crime; does not explain why social capital does not prevent everyone from committing crime.
Postmodern Criminology	Crime is an integral part of society.	Skeptical of science and scientific method; although it challenges other theories of crime prevention and control, it fails to offer feasible alternatives.
Peacemaking Criminology	Crime can be managed, not by stopping crime, but by making peace; citizens and social control agencies need to work together through education, social policies, human rights, and community involvement.	It is utopian and it fails to recognize the realities of law enforcement and crime control limitations.
Feminist Criminology	Men have dominated the field of criminal justice and have developed theories and written laws for the explanation and control of crime based on their own limited perspectives.	Inadequately accounts for crimes committed by females. Currently there is no single well-developed theory that explains female crime.

Wayne L. Davis, Ph.D. & Ann-Marie C. Buchanan, Ph.D.

Qualitative Studies

When studying a topic that cannot be quantitatively predicted, such as human emotions, qualitative studies are most effective. Indeed, qualitative studies are preferred for describing and interpreting experiences in context specific settings because each person's reality is construed in his or her own mind (Adams, 1999; Ponterotto, 2005). Feelings, opinions, and emotions cannot be accurately assessed via quantitative analysis; probing the participants for more detail through in-depth interviews using open-ended questions is required. Although there is no generally accepted guideline for data analysis in qualitative studies, the investigator may obtain software for content (data) analysis in order to identify themes in the data (Berg, 2007; Choi, Green, & Gilbert, 2011). Themes in the data provide meaning. Qualitative research attempts to reveal the meanings that participants have given to various phenomena. However, there are some limitations to qualitative studies. Because the sample size is often small and the experiences have occurred in context specific settings that are unique to each participant, the results cannot be generalized to a larger population. In addition, due to forgetfulness and intentional deception, experiences from the past may be reported less than accurate (McLeod, White, Mullins, Davey, Wakefield, & Hill, 2008). In short, qualitative studies ask **why** variables are related but not **how** they are related. For example, a qualitative research question may ask, *Why do you feel that ice cream sales are related to the murder rate?*

There are various ways to conduct qualitative research. The appropriate qualitative research design will depend on the purpose and focus of the study, and how the data will be collected and analyzed. See Table 5.

Table 5

Qualitative Research (Berg, 2007; Hatch, 2002; Leedy & Ormrod, 2016).

Qualitative Study Research Design	Purpose	Focus	Data Collection	Data Analysis
Phenomenological	To understand truth and reality from the participants' point of view	A specific event as perceived by an individual	Purposive sampling consisting of 5-25 individuals for in-depth and unstructured interviews	Identify common themes and synthesize them into an overall concept
Ethnography	To understand how the participants' behaviors reflect the culture of a group in a natural setting	A specific location where a group of people share a common culture	Artifact collection, participation observation, and structured and unstructured interviews	Identify underlying beliefs and phenomena and synthesize into a general behavior
Focus Group Study	To understand truth and reality from the participants' point of view	Specific events as perceived by a small group of individuals	Interviews and any other relevant data sources; Individuals who share common traits and experiences interact and provide data beyond what any single participant could provide; are most appropriate for	Identify common themes and synthesize into an overall concept; A weakness in this technique is that the group consensus may overshadow a particular individual's perspective.

			studies that are explanatory in nature.
Case Study	To understand one person or event in great detail because of the situation is poorly understood	One case in its natural environment or a few cases in their natural environment	Interviews, observation, written documents, and audiovisual information	Identify common themes and synthesize into an overall concept
Grounded Theory	To derive a theory by collecting and interpreting data in a natural setting in multiple stages	The process of human actions and interactions and how they impact each other	Interviews and any other relevant data sources	Prescribed and systematic way of coding the data; to identify interrelationships in the data in order to construct a theory
Content Analysis	To identify themes and patterns in a body of material through a systematic examination of the data	Any communication displayed in verbal, visual, or behavioral fashion.	Sampling the specific material to be analyzed and coding the material in a precisely defined manner.	Tabulation of the frequency of each coded theme for descriptive and inferential statistical analysis.

Qualitative Theme Analysis: Content Analysis

Qualitative research studies attempt to understand **why** events happen by discovering themes in the data. Because there is no generally accepted guideline for data analysis and display in qualitative studies, many different techniques for identifying themes in qualitative data may be utilized (Choi et al., 2011). Some of the techniques work better for short, open–ended responses while other techniques work better for rich, complex narratives. See Table 6 for several different techniques that may be used during **content analysis** to identify themes in qualitative data (Ryan & Bernard, n.d.).

Table 6

Content Analysis: Several Techniques to Identify Themes

General Technique	Specific Technique	Description
Analysis of Words	Word repetitions	Informal: Note unique words (and their synonyms) that are used often because they determine important ideas.
		Formal: count the number of times unique words are used to create a list of important ideas.
	Indigenous categories	Experience and expertise often use specialized vocabulary. Create categories by seeking terms that sound unfamiliar or are used in unfamiliar ways.
	Key-words-in-context	Look at how concepts are used. Identify key words and search the text to find all instances of how the words are used. Assess the immediate context. Themes are identified by sorting examples into piles of similar meaning.
Analysis of blocks of text	Compare and contrast	Conduct a line-by-line analysis to identify the idea in the current line and how the idea is similar or different from the previous line.
	Social science queries	Search for specific topics that may generate major social and cultural themes (e.g., managing interpersonal social relationships, informal methods of social control, achieving social status, etc.).
	Searching for missing information	Search for themes that are absent from the text. Silence may indicate a topic that the person is unwilling or afraid to discuss.
Intentional analysis of	Metaphors and analogies	Look for metaphors that produce patterns of underlying principles.

linguistic features	Transitions	Look for naturally occurring shifts in thematic content (new paragraphs in written text and pauses in oral speech).
	Connectors	Look for phrases that indicate relationships among topics (e.g. causal relationships, conditional relationships, time-oriented relationships, and spatial orientations).
Physical manipulation of text	Unmarked texts	Read the text several times, highlight different salient themes, and group similar themes. Then, in the remaining text, look for less obtrusive themes.
	Pawing	Read the text several times, separate the key phrases, and look for patterns in the data via the interocular percussion test.
	Cutting and sorting	Look for quotes that seem important; group similar quotes to identify themes. Good for identifying subthemes.

Content Analysis for Police Officers

Content analysis may be used by police officers to analyze both verbal and nonverbal information. For example, a police officer who stops a pickup truck may become suspicious that there are drugs in the vehicle if the suspects clinch their fists (they may be preparing to fight), if they take off their hats and sunglasses (they do not want to damage them during a fight), if they start whispering to one another (they may be making a plan of attack), if they try to keep certain parts of their bodies shielded from the officer (they may be trying to conceal weapons), if they start looking around (they may be looking for witnesses, weapons, or escape routes), and/or if they try to position the officer between them. Each of these clues may support the theme that violence is about to occur. Indeed, being able to recognize themes may save an officer's life.

Sampling

One of the most difficult barriers with conducting research is obtaining the data. Once the data are collected, analyses can easily be performed; the researcher can control the process. However, if the data cannot be collected, then the research study cannot be completed. Relying on others to provide data is risky and may be out of the researcher's control. For example, if the researcher plans to collect data from police officers on police department misbehavior, the department may not want to advertise actions that may lead to lawsuits and may block the researcher's opportunities to collect data. It may be a waste of time to complete a research proposal only to find that the data cannot be collected. Thus, a researcher should make sure at the outset of the study that the data can be collected. The data may be collected directly from first-hand experience by the researcher for the current study (primary data) or may be relevant to the current study but collected by someone else for another purpose (secondary data).

For a qualitative study, the participants must be capable of providing the sought-after data. There should be a reason for the manner in which potential participants are selected. Sometimes it may be important that the potential participants reside in a certain geographical location. Perhaps it is important to collect data from both sexes. Other times the potential participants may not be known in advance, such as drug dealers, and they may need to be found via other participants. See Table 7 for sampling designs.

Descriptive Statistics

Once the data are collected, descriptive statistical analyses will need to be performed. The descriptive statistics will check for patterns and trends in the data (Norusis, 2008). They provide an overview of the general nature of the data and may point out problems with the data.

Table 7

Sampling Designs (Balian, 1988; Field, 2005; Leedy & Ormrod, 2016)

Sampling Designs		
Probability Sampling	Simple random	Every member of the population has an equal chance of being selected.
	Stratified random	An equal number of participants in each group is selected and the individuals in each group have an equal chance of being selected.
	Proportional stratified	Individuals have an equal chance of being selected but in proportion to defined properties.
	Cluster	A large geographic area is divided into smaller units that are comprised of the same characteristics. All of the units are clustered together as the sample, and a subset of the cluster is randomly selected.
	Systematic	A sample is selected based on a predetermined sequence; method is accurate only if the listing is not biased in any way.
Nonprobability Sampling	Convenience	A sample that uses any participant who is willing and available to participate.
	Quota	A sample that seeks participants only until a pre-determined number is achieved.
	Purposive	A sample that is targeted according to particular criteria.
	Snow Ball	A sample in which one participant recommends other potential participants.

Examples of the Difference between a Quantitative and Qualitative Study

Example of Quantitative Study

Quantitative study: Many more people speed at 5:00 pm than at noon (a large problem exists but we have no idea **why** people are speeding around 5:00 pm). Although a problem has been identified, we would be guessing as to **why** the problem exists. Spending a lot of resources on a guess is risky and unwise. Perhaps people should be asked **why** they are speeding.

Example of Qualitative Study

Qualitative study: A mother speeds around 5:00 pm because she has kids at daycare and daycare closes at 5:15 pm (this is **why** a problem exists, but it is unclear if only a few people actually speed at 5:00 pm due to daycare issues; perhaps people speed for different reasons and this was a one-time event). It would be unwise to spend a lot of resources to fix the daycare problem based on one speeder's response.

Examples of Quantitative Research Questions

What is the relationship among the number of years that African American girls have participated in school-sponsored contact sports prior to graduating from high school, their childhood religiosity, and their amount of aggression as young adults?

Is there a significance difference between male and female athletes and their amount of religiosity?

Is there a relationship between age and emotional intelligence?

Examples of Qualitative Research Questions

What is your perception of how negative punishment in sports has influenced you as a parent?

What are the perceptions that adolescents have of their role models in determining their smoking status?

How do you feel that company policies have affected your work performance?

Why do you believe that the riot broke out?

How do you feel about affirmative action?

Examples of Assessing Various Types of Qualitative Data

The Message of Music

Local residents use music to communicate. Therefore, police officers need to pay attention to the music of minorities because their songs may be transmitting qualitative messages of how they perceive society. For example, there must be a reason why minorities sing songs about excessive police force. Perhaps they have experienced such events. Even if the officers do not believe these messages, the minorities may believe them. Hence, it is important for the police to listen to what the community members are saying and to understand their messages.

Example of Assessing Information in Love Songs

The lyrics for 10 love songs, which have all been ranked number one on the billboards, have been collected and examined (About. com: Country music, n.d.; AlaskaJim.com, 2007; Songfacts, n.d.; Songlyrics.com, n.d.). Five of the songs are performed by men and five are performed by women. The five songs performed by men include 1) *Pretty Woman*, by Roy Orbison, 2) *Daydream Believer*, by the Monkees, 3) *El Paso*, by Marty Robbins, 4) *Running Bear*, by Johnny Preston, and 5) *Hello, I Love You*, by the Doors. The five songs performed by women include 1) *I Will Always Love You*, by Dolly Parton, 2) *To Sir With Love*, by Lulu, 3) *Love Child*, by the Supremes, 4) *Will You Love Me Tomorrow?*, by the Shirelles, and 5) *Respect*, by Aretha Franklin. The songs performed by men will be compared to the songs performed by women by comparing themes between the lyrics. All of the lyrics performed for each sex will be combined and an overall comparison will be made.

The unit of analysis, which "is the amount of text that is assigned a code" (Neuman, 2006, p. 327), shall be the stanza. Furthermore, because the words "I love you," may actually mean, "I am infatuated with you and want sexual intercourse even though I do not know you," the theme of each stanza shall be evaluated by using latent coding. Indeed, latent coding may be more valid than manifest coding, which simply counts the number of times that the words appear. This means that the entire song must be read prior to any evaluations so that the overtone can be assessed. In addition, a stanza may include more than one theme. However, before a content analysis can commence, a list of variables needs to be developed (Sproull, 1995).

Variables:

1) Long term love – a long term commitment, perhaps as in marriage;
2) Infatuation – burning desire for immediate action;
3) Puppy Love –nonsexual and superficial;
4) Gain love – want other person to provide love;
5) Give love - willing to sacrifice oneself for love;
6) Believes superior to other person;
7) Believes subordinate to (i.e., worships) other person; and
8) Believes equal to other person.

Table 8

Summary of the 8 Variables for the Lyrics of 10 Love Songs.

Variable	# of times variable appeared (Men)	# of times variable appeared (Women)
1	9	17
2	17	1
3	1	0
4	5	2
5	9	4
6	0	1
7	8	6
8	6	5

According to Table 8, the overall themes of the songs indicate that men seem to be more interested in short term love than in long term relationships as compared to women. Furthermore, men seem to want women to submit themselves in love, and they are willing to die for it. Women, on the other hand, seem to want lasting relationships. Moreover, women sometimes are willing to submit themselves to men, but they may want something in exchange (e.g., respect).

Ethnography: Assessing Information in a Natural Setting

Date: Monday, November 2013
Location: Wana Cup Restaurant in Shipshewana, Indiana
Time: 11:00 am – 11:30 am

Ethnography seeks to describe a culture from the local or indigenous people's point of view (Berg, 2007). Data collection includes participant observation, participant interviewing, and artifact examination in order "to understand the cultural knowledge that group members use to make sense of the everyday experiences" (Hatch, 2002, p. 21). Thus, I entered a local Amish restaurant to observe customers.

Sense of Vision

As I pulled up to the restaurant, I observed one car parked in front of the restaurant and 4 horse-and-buggies parked on the side of the restaurant. All of the horses were either brown or black and all of the buggies were black. The car, on the other hand, was red. All of the lights on the outside of the restaurant were gas lanterns. The entire building was gray, even the roof top. Furthermore, there was a white wooden fence in front of the building. In short, there were no extravagant colors advertising this restaurant.

Once inside the building, I observed 8 customers: 4 men and 4 women. All of customers seemed to be between 50 and 60 years of age. The customers sat at two tables, 2 men and 2 women at each table. The men sat across from the women.

The men had some particular characteristics. First, all 4 of the men had full beards but none of them had mustaches. Second, none of them wore belts; instead, they all wore suspenders. Third, all 4 of the men wore dark blue pants, which appeared rugged, like workpants (they were not blue jeans). Fourth, all 4 of the men wore black coats, black boots, and black hats. Fifth, all 4 of the men wore eye glasses (versus contact lenses). Sixth, none of the men wore any jewelry.

The 4 women seemed to match the men that they accompanied. First, all four of the women wore black coats and white bonnets. Second, all of the women wore either black or blue dresses. In other words, the colors were conservative and they were not blue jeans. Third, all 4 of the women wore black boots and black stockings. Fourth, all of these women wore eye glasses (versus contact lenses). Fifth, all of the women had black purses. Sixth, none of the women wore any jewelry.

As far as the environment, I noticed that there was a wooden sign on the wall with the Lord's Prayer on it. This seemed to be significant; indeed, the men and women closed their eyes and seemed to pray before they ate. Furthermore, I noticed that the advertisement signs above the cash register were made of cardboard, although they did have professional looking drawings on them. For example, a banana split sign had a very good drawing of a banana split on it. In addition, the colors in the building were simple. The walls had wood paneling halfway up on them. Above that, the walls were white. Finally, the unisex bathroom utilized a single cloth roller towel (i.e., a single towel that everyone uses). Thus, all of the clues indicate that the restaurant is low tech.

Finally, I noticed that there was some money (unknown amount of dollar bills) resting on a tray on top of the garbage can. No one seemed to care that it sat there. This indicates that the people probably trust one another not to take it. The waitress finally picked the money up about 10 minutes later.

Sense of Smell

Sitting next to the group, I was overwhelmed by their bodily odor. Thus, it seems as though the individuals may not bathe daily. However, this odor did not seem to bother them.

Sense of Hearing

Except for the talking among the individuals, the inside of the restaurant was quiet. There was no music playing and there were no cell phones. In addition, the entire group appeared to speak a combination of German and English. However, when a man dressed in a suit approached them, they started speaking English to him.

Summary

In short, this culture is quite different than my culture. They do not desire modern technology and do not fancy materialistic products. Indeed, they do not even drive motor vehicles. However, they do seem to have strong social bonds within their community. Furthermore, they do not seem to be concerned about what outsiders think (as evidence by the Lord's Prayer on the wall).

Artifact Data: Assessing Information in Cemeteries

Greenwood Cemetery (Lagrange, Indiana)

Much unobtrusive actuarial data can be obtained in cemeteries (Berg, 2007). Greenwood Cemetery in Lagrange, Indiana is a public cemetery with thousands of grave sites. This cemetery does not have a policy requiring that flat stones be used. Consequently, there are many different types of headstones used in this cemetery. All of the headstones face east, a Christian tradition, and there is an overall Christian theme at the site (other religious denominations are not obvious) (Graves, 2006).

Headstones from 200 years ago

Greenwood Cemetery, a municipality cemetery, contains headstones with dates ranging from persons who fought in the American Revolutionary War until the present day. Most of the headstones for military personnel are similar to one another. They are about three feet high, white, and contain a cross at the top. A military headstone contains the name of the deceased, the state identifying where the person came from, the rank of the person during the war, the name of the war fought in, and the dates of birth and death. In many cases, the commanding officer's name is also included on the headstone. For example, one headstone reads as follows, "Abel Mattoon, Massachusetts, PVT, Capt. T. Williams Co, Revolutionary War, 1759-1837." Next to each of these headstones for military personnel is a metal rod, about two feet high, with a five point star on top of it with the word, "Comrade," on it.

Analysis – Basically, it appears that individuals in this era wanted to advertise great accomplishments. By listing the commanders' names on the headstones, it appears that these historic headstones allow for confirmation of the facts. In addition, by having crosses near the top of the headstones, the headstones appear to indicate loyalty to God and country.

Headstones from 100 years ago

Another section of the cemetery contains family plots. In one example, there are six headstones for one family. The one on the farthest right is a 10 foot high megalith, which looks like the Washington monument (Butterfield, 2003). Near the top are decorative images of diamonds. The front of this headstone reads, "In memory, father and mother." The back side states a name, the date died, and the age in years, months, and days; no actual date of birth is listed. The other five family members' headstones are to the left of the monument and are about two feet high and attached to one another via a concrete slab. For these, only names and dates are provided (e.g., Jacob Brown, 1829-1906). Of these five headstones, a male's name appears to be on both the farthest right and on the farthest left with three female names between them. Due to their relative positions to one another, it seems as though the females are being protected by the males. Many headstones in this era seem to describe men as independent human beings, but women are depicted as attached to men.

Analysis - Basically, headstones in this era describe women by their social relationships to men. Many times, a woman's headstone lists her name, wife of [man's name], and dates of birth and death. However, the headstones of men do not describe the men's social relationships to women. Although most of these headstones have symbols on them, such as crosses, a hand holding the Bible, doves, and a variety of flowers (e.g., roses or Easter lilies), the text on them is brief.

Headstones from about 25 years ago

More recent headstones appear to be custom designed by making use of laser and digital technologies (Heller, 2008). Indeed, recent headstones in Greenwood Cemetery contain photographs, images, and text statements. For example, one young female who passed away in 1990 has her photograph in the center of the headstone, a fraternity emblem on the left side, an image of a swimmer on the right side, a Southwest Allen County Fire Department emblem at the bottom, and four statements from loved ones on the back. These statements include, "My darling Allison, God gave me the most precious gift in the world, it was you. You will always be with me in my heart, love always, Mom," and "To Allison, though lovers be lost, love shall not. Death shall have no dominion, Mike." In this section of the cemetery, headstones often have marriage dates on them with symbolic pictures (e.g., wedding rings interlocked or two hands holding one another), the name of the spouse, the names of children, etches of recreational activities (e.g., fishing), occupations (e.g., a tractor-trailer), and they are surrounded by urns, flowers, solar lights (which represent the eternal flame), and statues of pets, such as dogs.

Analysis – Basically, these headstones seem to describe family unity, social memberships, personal accomplishments, recreational activities, occupations, and pets. Furthermore, many of them contain colored photographs of the deceased, which can provide valuable physical characteristics. At the same time, crosses, angels, and doves indicate a Christian atmosphere.

Headstones from about 15 years ago

There is a baby section of headstones that date about the year 2000. On these headstones are words like, "our little angel," and "forever in our hearts." Moreover, surrounding these headstones is an abundance of angels, Easter bunnies, toys, crosses, flowers, and bears in the form of angels.

Analysis – The atmosphere seems to suggest a spiritual connotation where parents are trying to assure that their children are cared for and protected. In other words, the babies are not alone. Indeed, this area is heavily visited.

Eastbaren Cemetery (Shipshewana, Indiana)

Because there are many Amish in Lagrange County, Indiana, Eastbaren Cemetery, a private Amish cemetery with about 200 grave sites, was also examined. Every headstone in this cemetery is less than two feet high and all but four are white. The older headstones (in the 1800 era), simply state names and dates of birth and death. If marriages were involved, the spouse's name with the words "wife of" or "husband of" may be included on the headstones. More recent headstones (dated in the 1970s) may include the names of surviving family members on them (e.g., loving mother of James and Sara) along with bible verses on the back. For example, the back of one headstone reads, "Fear not little flock; for it is your father's good pleasure to give you the kingdom. Luke 12:32." Several headstones dated in the 1990s have both male and female names on them along with marriage dates.

About 10% of the grave markers in this cemetery simply state a name and date. In one case, there is a wooden cross made of weathered barn siding with a date of 2008. On this cross is a handwritten message made with a black marker that states, "What a great sacrifice so others can live," and "we miss you."

Analysis - Basically, this cemetery seeks simplicity and uniformity. There are no flowers, urns, photographs, solar lights, or statues. There are just headstones and crosses. Although some social statuses are indicated (e.g., wife of), significant others are listed (e.g., surviving family members' names), and significant events recorded (e.g., wedding dates), the atmosphere seems to focus on the afterlife and not on personal accomplishments in life. This is a sharp contrast to the Greenwood Cemetery.

Example: Focus Group Study

Focus group interviews, where individuals who share common traits and experiences interact and provide data beyond what any single participant could provide, are most appropriate for studies that are explanatory in nature (Hatch, 2002). However, a weakness in this technique is that the group consensus may overshadow a particular individual's perspective (Berg, 2007; Hatch). Following is a focus group study on police profiling.

The topic of discussion is community members' perceptions of police profiling.

Following is a statement of the basic rules (Berg, 2007). The discussion will be conducted in a polite and professional manner. Indeed, different points of view and experiences will provide an overall understanding of the issue. Therefore, all opinions are valued. A question will be asked, each participant will be asked to provide a short response, and then the question will be open for group discussion. Everyone is encouraged to respond.

Five open-ended questions will be asked during the interviews. The five questions are listed below.

- What is your perception of the relationship between the police and community?
- What is your perception of the relationship between the police and minorities?
- What is your perception of the relationship between minorities and whites?
- What is your experience with police profiling or racial discrimination?
- Do you think that the police have earned your respect? Explain.

Probe questions

Does the community support the police or is there constant conflict? Explain.
Do community members file a lot of complaints against officers? Explain.

Are there gangs in the area? Explain.

Do the police effectively serve minorities? Explain.
Are minorities adequately represented in local police? Explain.

Do minorities and whites struggle over political power? Explain.
Are minorities adequately represented in local courts? Explain.

Can you provide an example of a profiling experience? Explain.

Why do you trust the police? Explain.
Why do you not trust the police? Explain.
Have you ever had an encounter with a rude (or polite) police officer? Explain.

In order to gather a general feeling of civilians' perceptions of the local police, a focus group interview was conducted involving 7 participants. The interview was conducted in a room at a local university. The ground rules were described to the participants as 1) a question will be asked, 2) each participant will be asked to provide a short response, and 3) the question will then be open for group discussion (Berg, 2007). The seven participants are as follows: 1) O. Zing, a 32 year old Asian American female who was born in China; 2) L. Cloud, a 50 year old Native American female; 3) P. Cheddar, a 50 year white male, retired from the U.S. Army; 4) O. Twinkles, a 50 year old white female with 9 years of business experience; 5) T. Witne, a 50 year old white female with 5 years of manufacturing experience; 6) P. Proud, a 50 year old white female and homemaker;

and 7) L. Rodriguez, a 41 year old Hispanic female who was born in Panama. It should be noted that all of the participants who have stated that they are 50 years of age are probably not actually 50. Three of the females did not want to provide their actual ages. They simply stated "50 plus or minus." In short, the focus group participants are from different backgrounds and are able to provide different perspectives about the topic. Below is the essence of what the focus group participants stated.

Research Question: *What is your perception of the relationship between the police and community?*

"In general, the community does not respect the local and state police because the police are idiots. In fact, one state police officer was forced to resign because he is a thief" (P. Cheddar, personal communications of September 22, 2011). Because this event was advertised in the local media, the case being described is common knowledge for the group. Thus, all participants agreed with this statement.

Research Question: *What is your perception of the relationship between the police and minorities?*

"The police do profile. Anyone who is dark they profile. My son was walking with two blond hair boys. A cop pulled up to them and questioned them about smoking. The cop let the two blond hair boys go but made my son empty out his pockets to prove that he did not have any cigarettes" (L. Cloud, personal communications of September 22, 2011). Although all of the Caucasians in this group stated that they have had no personal experiences with the police, the Native American, the Chinese American, and the Hispanic American stated that they are aware of police discrimination against minorities. Only one female Caucasian stated that she believes discrimination occurs against minorities, but only because of what she has seen in the movies.

Research Question: *What is your perception of the relationship between minorities and whites?*

"Some minorities exaggerate ethnic problems. Some Chinese do not like to talk to whites because they do not think that whites like them. I say, how would they know until they talk with them? People feel comfortable talking to those who look similar" (O. Zing, personal communications of September 22, 2011). Zing also stated that several years ago at Indiana University, a Chinese American mom had a sick 12 year old son. She let her son sleep with her so that she could take care of him. Zing stated that this is common practice in China. However, social workers came, they charged the mom with sexual abuse, and they took her son away; consequently, her son, shortly thereafter, died. Zing stated that whites need to learn different cultural practices. The general consensus of the group is that whites do not communicate well with other cultures. The rest of the group backed this up with another example. They stated that, just a little while ago, there was an accident nearby and a Hispanic was killed. No one in the area knew how to speak Spanish and no one could communicate with the victim's family. Thus, the entire group claimed that there is definitely a communication problem between cultures.

Research Question: *What is your experience with police profiling or racial discrimination?*

"I only know what I have seen on T.V. and in the movies. White police officers pick on minorities" (P. Proud, personal communications of September 22, 2011). The overall consensus is that the participants have had no personal experience with police profiling or racial discrimination and that they have learned their perceptions through second-hand information. Only the Hispanic female may have actually experienced a profiling incident. In her case, she stated that she had pulled into a grocery store and that a white male city police officer started staring her down (L. Rodriguez, personal communications of September 22, 2011). She stated that after she left the store, about 20 minutes later, the officer followed her for about 4 miles out of the city. He then pulled her over and gave her a bogus excuse.

Research Question: *Do you think that the police have earned your respect?*

"I respect the police out of fear" (O. Zing, personal communications of September 22, 2011). The overall consensus is that those who respect the police do it because of the officers' position, not because of the officers' behaviors. Overall, it appears that all of the participants believe there are police-community concerns. Only the minority females, however, specifically believe that there are police-minority concerns. Finally, the group consensus is that the police are respected only because of their position of authority and not because of their behaviors.

Example: Case Study

Case studies can be performed in many types of social environments and can provide rich, in-depth information on simple or complex phenomenon (Berg, 2007). Indeed, case studies are effective in performing qualitative research on a person, a process, an institution, an event, a program, or a social group involving a contextualized contemporary (as opposed to historic) phenomenon within specified parameters (Hatch, 2002).

Case studies are among of the most popular research designs in law enforcement today (Champion, 2006). Case studies allow for thorough investigations of individuals in specific social settings and include detailed behavioral and psychological descriptions of persons in those settings. Because there are philosophical, political, and ethical issues involving police officer behaviors, a qualitative case study would be effective in understanding how police officers develop their attitudes. Indeed, a case study, which focuses on very few participants (perhaps only one participant), can provide the in-depth, detailed information that is necessary to understand police behavior (Berg, 2007). Furthermore, case studies allow formal interviews to supplement observations (Hatch, 2002).

There are five advantages to case studies (Champion, 2006). First, case studies are flexible and they allow the researcher to collect data via multiple techniques, such as observation, interviewing, and examination of records. Second, this flexibility can be extended to virtually any dimension. Third, case studies can be performed in many types of social environments. Fourth, case studies can be inexpensive if the researcher collects the data firsthand. Finally, a longitudinal case study will allow behavioral changes to be measured at specific points in time. This may be important if the incremental changes are small.

There are two disadvantages in performing case studies (Champion, 2006). First, case studies may not be generalized to larger populations. Because the research design is qualitative in nature, it is subjective and depends on how each person perceives truth and reality (Weber, 2004). Second, findings from case studies may not always support theories. In other words, the findings may not be conclusive proof of anything. Therefore, an accumulation of case studies is important in investigating similar phenomena so that confident statements can be made about the social world.

Personal Interview with State Police Officer (name changed for anonymity)

Y. Bell – State Police (personal communication on October 1, 2011)
Black/male 45 years old, born in U.S.
6 years corrections, 14 years police
About half of life lived in the city, half in the country

Research Question: What is your perception of the relationship between the police and the community?

Response: The community generally does not like the police. Many people are involved with some sort of crime, whether it be smoking marijuana or underage drinking, therefore they do not want the police to know their business. They only want the police when they need help. The community members in general, both blacks and whites, do not generally like the police department. If there is a shooting for example, whites will support the police and blacks will claim racism and oppose whites.

Research Question: What is your perception of the relationship between minorities and the police in your community?

Response: The police department absolutely profiles. White officers will pull black drivers over simply because of race. Many blacks get tired of this.

Research Question: What is your perception of the relationship between minorities and whites in your community?

Response: Anytime a shooting happens, white and blacks will divide. This is due to economic reasons and because of the racism the blacks perceive that whites practice against them.

Research Question: What is your experience with profiling or racial discrimination?

Response: I do not profile based on race or gender but I do profile behaviors. For example, when I pull up next to a driver and he will not look at me but looks straight forward with both hands on the steering wheel, this is suspicious behavior and I will look for valid reasons to pull the driver over. Also, one night several years ago, I was driving home from the gym and a county police officer was in the crossover with his headlights shining across the roadway. I was in an unmarked police car and wearing a do-rag on my head. As soon as I passed him, I knew that he was going to pull out and stop me, even though traffic was heavy. Sure enough, he pulled out and stopped me. I immediately showed him my police badge and asked him why he stopped me. He stated that I was weaving a little bit. That was untrue but I did not argue with him.

Research Question: Do you respect the police?

Response: Because I work with police officers, I trust them. We share a common experience. However, I do not trust the administration. The police department does not like complaints and will give too much credence to civilians and totally distrust the officers.

REFERENCES

About.com: Country music (n.d.). *Dolly Parton – Jolene.* Retrieved from http://countrymusic.about.com/od/cdreviewsmz/fr/Jolene.htm

Adams, W. (1999). The interpermeation of self and world: Empirical research, existential phenomenology, and transpersonal psychology. *Journal of Phenomenological Psychology, 30* (2), 39-65.

AlaskaJim.com (2007). *Top songs of the 1960's.* Retrieved from http://www.alaskajim.com/polls/2002topsongs1960s_results.htm

Balian, E. (1988). *How to design, analyze, and write doctoral or master's research* (2nd ed.). New York, NY: University Press of America.

Berg, B. (2007). *Qualitative research methods for the social sciences* (6th ed.). Boston, MA: Pearson Education, Inc.

Butterfield, A. (2003). Monuments and memorials. *New Republic, 228*(4), 27-32.

Champion, D. (2006). *Research methods for criminal justice and criminology* (3rd ed.). Upper Saddle River, NJ: Pearson Merrill Prentice Hall.

Choi, J.J., Green, D.L., & Gilbert, M.J. (2011). Putting a human face of crimes: A qualitative study on restorative justice processes for youths. *Child and Adolescent Social Work Journal, 28*(5), 335-355. doi: 10.1007/s10560-011-0238-9.

Corrigan, R. (2006). Making meaning of Megan's law. *Law & Social Inquiry, 31*(2), 267-312.

Davis, W.L. (2015). *Police community relations: Bridging the gap.* Bloomington, IN: Xlibris.

Fay, B. (1987). *Critical social science.* Ithaca, NY: Cornell University Press.

Field, A. (2005). *Discovering statistics using SPSS* (2nd ed.). Thousand Oaks, CA: Sage.

Graves 'will be allowed to face east' (2006 September 26). *Europe Intelligence Wire.*

Hatch, J. (2002). *Doing qualitative research in education settings.* Albany, NY: State University of New York Press.

Heller, S. (2008). Death, be not staid. *Print,* 62(4), 90-95.

Leedy, P. D. & Ormrod, J. E. (2016). *Practical Research: Planning and design (11th ed.).* Upper Saddle River, NJ: Prentice-Hall, Inc.

Lutterman, B. (2015). *Quantitative = Qualitative.* Assistant Professor of Visual Art at Lincoln Memorial University.

McLeod, K., White, V., Mullins, R., Davey, C., Wakefield, M., and Hill, D. (2008). How do friends influence smoking uptake? Findings from qualitative interviews with identical twins. *Journal of Genetic Psychology, 169* (2), 117-132.

Neuman, W. (2006). *Social research methods: Qualitative and quantitative approaches* (6th ed.). Boston, MA: Pearson Education, Inc.

Norusis, M.J. (2008). *SPSS 16.0 guide to data analysis.* Upper saddle River, NJ: Prentice Hall.

Ponterotto, J. (2005). Qualitative research in counseling psychology: A primer on research paradigms and philosophy of science. *Journal of Counseling, 52*(2), 126-136.

Ryan, G.W., & Bernanrd, H.R. (n.d.). *Techniques to identify themes in qualitative data*. Retrieved from http://www.analytictech.com/mb870/readings/ryan-bernard_techniques_to_identify_themes_in.htm

Schmalleger, F. (2011). *Criminology: A brief introduction*. Boston, MA: Prentice Hall

Songfacts (n.d.). *To sir with love*. Retrieved from http://www.songfacts.com/detail.php?id=2780

Songlyrics.com (n.d.). Retrieved from http://www.songlyrics.com/

Sower, C., & Gist, G.T. (1994). *Formula for change: Using the urban experiment station methods and the normative sponsorship theory*. East Lansing, MI: Michigan State University Press.

Sower, C., Holland, J., Tiedke, K., & Freeman, W. (1957). *Community Involvement: The webs of formal and informal ties that make for action*. Glencoe, IL: The Free Press.

Sproull, N. (1995). *Handbook of research methods: A guide for practitioners and students in the social sciences* (2nd ed.). Lanham, MD: The Scarecrow Press, Inc.

Turvey, B. E., & Petherick, W. (2009). *Forensic victimology: Examining violent crime victims in investigative and legal contexts*. Burlington, MA: Academic Press.

Weber, R. (2004). The rhetoric of positivism versus interpretivism: A personal view. *MIS Quarterly 28*(1), iii-xii.

Wakefield, J. (1995). When an irresistible epistemology meets an immovable ontology. *Social Work Research, 19* (1).

CHAPTER 2. ETHICS IN RESEARCH

In order to protect participants, all university researchers must obtain the approval of the Institutional Review Board (IRB) prior to gathering participant data (Berg, 2007). This is a federal law. The purpose of the Institutional Review Board (IRB) and approval process is to ensure the ethical treatment and protection of human research participants and/or their records. Researchers must comply with principles of the Belmont Report, federal guidelines, and professional societies and organizations (e.g., American Education Research Association, Academy of Management, American Counseling Association, and American Psychological Association).

The Institutional Review Board (IRB) helps guarantee that human participants are protected by requiring that all researchers associated with a university obtain IRB approval prior to any interactions with participants. This policy is important because it provides for an objective, neutral party to evaluate the research proposal and to provide unbiased recommendations, which help protect the participants. Although there may be some risk of harm in any research project, this risk must be identified and evaluated prior to the research commencing. Furthermore, the participants must be made aware of any potential risks. Indeed, if the researchers are secretive, then they will lose credibility and this may negatively impact future research. In addition, the researchers should debrief the participants after the study and make counseling available to those participants who need it (Berg, 2007).

In order to inform potential researchers of the appropriate federal guidelines involving research, universities that conduct research offer training modules on informed consent, on assessing risk, and on privacy and confidentiality. In some cases, the participants, such as pregnant women, may be vulnerable. Indeed, the fetuses within their bodies must be protected. Thus, researchers must be aware of potential concerns so that they may design their research projects appropriately.

When children are participants, there are two types of informed consent: active and passive. Active informed consent is the formal written permission of an informed parent or legal guardian who allows their children to partake in a research study (Berg, 2007). However, many times parents and legal guardians fail to return signed consent forms, resulting in poor response rates. This is not to say that the parents and legal guardians are denying the participation of their children in the studies. Many times, they just simply fail to respond.

In order to avoid excluding relevant young participants in a study, researchers often use passive informed consent (Berg, 2007). Passive informed consent assumes that the parents and legal guardians grant permission for their children to participate in a study if they do not return a refusal form after being informed about the study. Passive informed procedures often do not fully inform parents and legal guardians about a research study or give them amply opportunities to refuse. It is assumed that the parents and legal guardians are not refusing to allow their children to participate if they do not say no. However, if parents and legal guardians do not respond due to lackadaisical parental attitudes, they may not necessarily be saying yes. Thus, this is an ethical concern that must be considered.

See Table 9 for an example of an institutional review board checklist.

Table 9

Institutional Review Board – Checklist

Done	Items
	1. Research Description
	• Research hypotheses, questions, and purpose
	• Research procedures
	• Instruments
	• Adequacy of resources to protect and accommodate participants
	2. Research Setting
	• Description of research settings
	• Research sites' IRB information
	• Approval for access
	• Contact information for the research sites
	3. Participant Population and Sample
	• Number and ages of participants
	• Special groups
	• Inclusion criteria and rationale
	• Excluded populations
	4. Participant Recruitment
	• Recruitment methods
	• Recruitment incentives
	5. Risks
	• Classification of risk
	• Explanation of risk classification
	• Participant protections and risk mitigation
	6. Benefits
	7. Privacy & Confidentiality
	8. Informed Consent
	9. Conflict of Interest
	10. Supplemental Forms
	• Risk Assessment Addendum
	• Pregnant Women, Fetuses, etc.
	• Prisoners
	• Children
	• Vulnerable Population (e.g., cognitively impaired)
	• Request for a Waiver of Elements of Informed Consent Form
	• Internet-Based Research
	• Records-Based Research
	• Disclosure of Financial Interest
	• Certification of Translation
	• IRB Training Records
	• Approval Letters Granting Access to Sites and/or Participants
	• Informed Consent Document
	• Instruments, Surveys, or Other Research Documents
	• Recruitment brochures, flyers, scripts, etc.
	• Other:

Examples of Addressing Ethical Issues

Guidelines that govern how human participants should be treated in research are based on the 1979 Belmont Report, which was published by the National Commission for the Protection of Human Subjects of Biomedical and Behavioral Research (Berg, 2007; Zimmerman, 1997). The Belmont Report has established ethical principles to guide researchers' conduct when they collect data from human participants. Even if the risks for the participants in the study are minimal, the researcher needs to take measures to ensure that the participants will be protected throughout the entire study. Below are examples of ethical issues that were addressed during a correlational research study involving a) religiosity and school-sponsored contact sport participation and b) aggressive behaviors later in life (Davis, 2014).

Budget

The researcher has disclosed the cost of the study and the source of the funds to the Institutional Review Board. First, it is important to know if the study is financially feasible. Second, it is important to know that a third party is not influencing the researcher's interpretation of the study's findings via its financial support.

Researcher's Position Statement

The researcher has played contact sports from fourth grade through twelfth grade. Although the researcher believes that contact sports may teach some children anti-social behaviors, the researcher also believes that contact sports may teach some children pro-social behaviors. Consequently, the researcher will be open-minded and will interpret the study's data objectively. Furthermore, the researcher is currently a police officer who enforces laws involving aggressive behaviors. Although the researcher has no personal interest in the participants, who will be recruited from local colleges and universities, the researcher will protect the participants' anonymity by disassociating their names from the instruments.

Protection from Harm

To help ensure that the participants are not harmed, the researcher will obtain an Institutional Review Board approval prior to gathering data (Berg, 2007). Furthermore, the researcher will collect data from the participants in a comfortable and secure place. If the participants feel uneasy, especially if their responses are sensitive, then they may withhold valuable data.

Potential Negative Risks

Because the study will ask questions about aggression, there is the chance that negative emotions may be generated. Therefore, the researcher will provide the participants with counselor information so that troubled participants may seek assistance. In addition, the researcher will respect the research sites and will keep any disturbances to a minimum.

Informed Consent & Assurance of Volunteerism

Informed consent provides the participants with information on the purpose of the study, the procedures, and the potential risks (Creswell, 2009). As a result, the participants will be able to make informed decisions on whether they want to consent and to participate in the study. Because the participants' safety take precedence over all else, the researcher will make it quite clear to the participants that they may withdraw from the study at any time without consequence. Indeed, their participation is voluntary.

Confidentiality & Anonymity

The researcher will protect the confidentiality of participant information throughout the entire study. Personal information about participants will be secured to prevent the loss and misuse of data; completed surveys will only be accessible to the research team and will not be shared with anyone else. After the data from the surveys have been analyzed, the researcher will secure the data in a locked safe until it is time to be destroyed. Furthermore, the researcher will clearly claim ownership of the data in order to avoid any misunderstandings about who controls the data. Although the researcher will protect the participants' personal information, there is a risk that any collected data could be subpoenaed by a court.

The researcher will protect the anonymity of the participants. For example, in order to help protect the participants' identities, the researcher will contact professors at local colleges and universities and have them distribute a letter of invitation to potential participants. If students are willing to participate in the study, then they will respond to the letter and contact the researcher. Second, because knowing the identities of the participants is not crucial to the study, there is no need for the participants to place their names on the surveys.

Honesty with Professionalism

Ethical guidelines will be followed during the writing and dissemination of the data (Creswell, 2009). First, the paper will be written using nonbiased language. Second, the data will be complete, unadulterated, and the researcher will make a clear distinction between the evidence and the researcher's interpretation of the evidence. Third, no one will be allowed to use the data to take advantage of another person. Finally, the study's findings will be open to public review, which will enhance its credibility.

Reducing Anxiety

In order to reduce the participants' anxieties, the researcher will effectively communicate with the participants. For example, the researcher will provide a letter of introduction prior to the study as a way to promote its legitimacy (Creswell, 2009). The researcher will make the study's purpose and benefits known to all participants. In addition, the researcher will make the participants aware of the study's process so that they will know what to expect. In short, clear communication will promote the credibility of the study and reduce the participants' anxieties.

Autonomous Agents

The study will be designed so that participants are considered autonomous agents. For example, factors that may indicate the participants are autonomous agents include a) whether the participants are at least 21 years of age, b) whether they are free to act on their own judgments on whether or not to participate, and c) whether they have previously indicated an interest in participating in the study. Furthermore, an informed consent form describes the purpose of the study, the benefits, and the potential risks (Creswell, 2003). As a result, the participants will be able to make informed decisions on whether or not they want to participate in the study. A statement will make it quite clear to the participants that they can withdraw from the study at any time without consequence. Thus, their decision to participate will be informed, will be voluntary, and will require a signature.

Implied Consent via Electronic Signature

Before electronic data are collected from a participant, the individual will be required to provide an electronic signature of consent (Post, 2008). A signature of consent may be obtained electronically by integrating it into the informed consent form. For example, the electronic consent form may provide information on a) the researcher, b) volunteer participation, c) data storage, d) compensation, e) benefits, f) risks, g) confidentiality, h) legal rights, i) contact information, and j) how to exit the study, if so desired. In addition, if the potential participant agrees to participate in the study, then the participant will be required to click on the link that clearly indicates her consent to participate in the study. If an individual does click on the link that indicates willingness to participate in the study, then consent as a willing participant in the study will be implied. In this case, the participant will be allowed to complete the questionnaire. However, if an individual does not want to participate in the study, then the person will click on the link that clearly indicates unwillingness to participate in the study. Consequently, if the individual declines to participate in the study, then the person will be denied access to the questionnaire. Furthermore, a participant should be able to exit the study at any time before data are electronically submitted.

In short, ethical standards will be followed in three specific areas. These three areas are the data collection process, the analysis and interpretation of the data, and the writing and dissemination of the report (Creswell, 2003). See Table 10 for an ethics checklist.

Table 10

Ethics Checklist for Data Collection, Data Analysis, and Writing of Report

Ethics Checklist

<u>Data Collection Process</u>

_Participation is voluntary

_Purpose understood by participants, including benefits

_Process understood by participants

_Participants' privacy safeguarded – data collected confidentially

_Appropriate signatures obtained – from participants

_Appropriate permission obtained – from data collection site

_Research site respected

<u>Analysis and Interpretation of Data</u>

_Participants' anonymity safeguarded – names not attached to surveys

_Ownership of data declared

_Data put into storage for 7 years – only shared with study team

<u>Writing and Dissemination of the Study</u>

_Use of nonbiased language

_Unadulterated data

_Proper use of data

_Credibility of study confirmed by readers

University Research – Best Practices for Research

Below are **general practices** for qualitative research. These general practices are necessary in order to effectively investigate and present a qualitative study.

General Practices for Qualitative Research

1) In order to protect participants, all university researchers must obtain the approval of the Institutional Review Board (IRB) prior to gathering participant data (Berg, 2007). This is a federal law.

2) The researcher must describe the topic of the qualitative research in an interesting manner. For example, the study's aim and purpose must be clear and important in order to gain the attention of potential participants. Otherwise, many individuals may ignore the study.

3) The researcher must consider the availability of the data before the researcher commits to a study. If the data are controlled by the government, for example, and the information is sensitive, then the data might not be available for analysis. Individuals may simply refuse to participate in the study.

4) The researcher must establish the need for a qualitative study (Seale, Gobo, Gubrium, & Silverman, 2004). Qualitative studies provide thorough investigations of individuals in specific social settings and include detailed behavioral and psychological descriptions of persons in those settings (Champion, 2006). These findings may not be generalized to other populations (Creswell, 2009). If predictions are needed and generalizations to larger populations are required, then quantitative techniques should be investigated.

5) The researcher must select the proper kind of qualitative research to be performed (Hatch, 2002). Each qualitative research method is designed to obtain information in a different way. Thus, a research question may be better answered by a particular kind of qualitative research method. For example, a longitudinal case study may be better in

assessing incremental changes over time than will a focus group interview. Align the method of research with the research question.

6) A researcher must have an open mind and must be willing to interpret data that are unexpected and contrary to personal beliefs (Seale et al., 2004). The participants are being studied, not the researcher.

7) The researcher must present authentic findings (Creswell, 2009). The researcher must not fudge the data; otherwise, the researcher will have no credibility and the study will be questionable. Indeed, perhaps the significance of the study will indicate that other variables exist that affect the results.

8) The researcher must make a clear distinction between the evidence and the interpretation of the evidence (Seale et al., 2004). This is important because to mix the two is misleading and less than ethical. The goal is to provide legitimate information; it is not to try to trick someone.

9) The researcher needs to select the appropriate participants for the study. For example, if police officers are the subject of study, then investigate police officers. A purposive sampling is appropriate for a difficult-to-reach, specialized population (Neuman, 2006).

Below are **specific practices** for qualitative research. These practices are important in carrying out a qualitative study.

Specific Practices for Qualitative Research

1) The researcher needs to record the evidence as accurately as possible. Video tape the data (e.g., interviews) if possible because this will provide a more complete visual and audio

account. Always supplement the data collection process with note-taking, just in case a problem develops with the audio-visual equipment.

2) For a qualitative one-on-one interview, the researcher needs to develop a question that is open-ended and allows for in-depth answers (Creswell, 2009). Qualitative studies seek to understand the meanings, concepts, symbols, and characteristics of things. Thus, this requires narrative style answers. In addition, develop probe questions for further elaboration.

3) The researcher needs to protect the participants (Berg, 2007). The researcher needs to follow ethical guidelines and to protect the privacy and confidentiality of the participants by explaining the research process to them and by obtaining their permission to proceed.

4) The researcher needs to perform a literature review (Balian, 1988). The goal is to add to the body of knowledge. Gaps in the knowledge will not be known unless prior studies are examined. Otherwise, the study may be meaningless, especially if the topic has already been exhausted.

5) The researcher needs to use triangulation (Creswell, 2009). This will help validate the data and may provide additional insights or generate additional questions. There are several ways to use triangulation in research (Berg, 2007). These include data triangulation, investigator triangulation, theory triangulation, and methodological triangulation. All help enhance the validity of the study.

6) The researcher needs to obtain the proper software for content (data) analysis and needs to practice using it to identify themes (Berg, 2007). The software is only useful

if it is used in the right manner. Free qualitative software packages are available on the Internet and the researchers should familiarize themselves with what is available.

7) During interviews, the researcher needs to keep the participants focused on the topic. The data sought should seek to answer the research question. Because the amount of raw data can be overwhelming, the researcher should continually evaluate whether the data are related to the question. This will allow the researcher to manage the huge amount of data. Do not get side-tracked.

8) The researcher needs to interview the participants in a comfortable and secure place (Berg, 2007). If the participants are afraid that someone may overhear their responses, especially if those responses are sensitive and may get them into trouble, then they may withhold valuable information.

9) The researcher needs to be flexible (Berg, 2007). Adjust personal schedules to meet with the participants. After all, they are going out of their way to provide data, so personal schedules may have to be adjusted to meet the participants when they are available.

10) The researcher needs to dress appropriately (Berg, 2007). If the researcher fails to dress professionally, then the participants may doubt the quality of the study and the confidentiality of the data. The image of the researcher may reflect the quality of the study.

11) For focus group interviews, use a round table so that all of the participants can be observed. Otherwise, valuable information may be missed.

Purpose of Informed Consent Form

Before data are collected from a participant, ethical standards require that the researcher obtain informed consent from the participant. The main purpose of the form is to provide information that may affect the participant's decision about whether or not the person wants to participate in the research project. The potential participant must sign the informed consent form before data are collected from the person. However, it is possible to obtain implied consent if the data are collected over the Internet. If data are collected over the Internet, the researcher will need the participant to actively click on a link that indicates that the person is willing to participate in the study.

The informed consent form will answer the following questions.

1. Who is conducting the research?
2. What does participation involve?
3. Why is the person being asked to participate?
4. What are the risks involved?
5. Will the participant realize any benefits?
6. What will happen if new information becomes available during the study that may impact the person's decision to participate?
7. How will confidentiality be protected?
8. What are the consequences if the participant withdraws from the study?
9. What is the cost to the participant?
10. Will the participant be compensated for illness or injury?
11. Will the participant show consent by providing a signature?

In addition, if any type of health or medical information is sought, a HIPAA form will be required. On the next several pages are examples of an **Invitation Letter,** a **HIPAA Form,** and an **Informed Consent Form**.

Example of Electronic Invitation Letter

Invitation to Participate in Research Study

A Correlational Study of Childhood Religiosity,
Childhood Sport Participation, and Sport-Learned
Aggression Among African American Female Athletes

Participants are needed for a research study in order to gain insight on the relationships among childhood religiosity, childhood sport participation, and sport-learned aggression. The research cannot be performed without data. Your participation is voluntary and provides that data. Your name will not be written on the questionnaires. The survey site will be active for three weeks.

You are being invited to participate in this study because you are a member of Zoomerang and because you match the characteristics of the population. The population of interest is African American females, 21 to 40 years of age. However, in order to gain control over the study's variables, there are several other conditions that must be satisfied in order to participate in the study. You must meet the all of the qualifications listed below in order to participate in this study. If you do not meet all of the qualifications listed below, please exit the study. Because the study requires that the participants have not been medically treated for depression or diagnosed with Attention Deficit Disorder, a health information release form will be required.

Various Types of Sports (for reference)

Contact Sports	Collision Sports	Non-Contact Sports
a) Volleyball	a) Football	a) swimming
b) Basketball	b) Wrestling	b) tennis
c) Soccer	c) Boxing	c) track
d) Lacrosse	d) gymnastics	
e) Water Polo	e) softball	

Qualifications to Participate

a) You must be an African American female.

b) You must be 21 to 40 years of age.

c) You must have attended U.S. secondary schools.

d) You must have graduated from high school.

e) You must not have been medically treated for depression.

f) You must not have been diagnosed with Attention Deficit Disorder.

g) You must not have played collision sports in secondary school.

h) You may have been a non-athlete and may never have played sports in secondary school.

i) You may have played non-contact sports in secondary school. This will not impact the number of years that you have played contact sports.

j) If you have played contact sports in secondary school, then you must have played in 12th grade.

k) If you have played contact sports in 12th grade, then you must have not skipped a grade level of participation once you started to play. In other words, you must not have had any discontinuity in contact sport participation from grade level to grade level, starting from the time when you first engaged in school-sponsored contact sports. For example, if you first started to play school-sponsored contact sports in 7th grade, then you must have played in 7th, 8th, 9th, 10th, 11th, and 12th grades. However, if you first started to play school-sponsored contact sports in 11th grade, then you must have played only in 11th and 12th grades.

If you meet the above conditions, then please respond to this letter of invitation and take the survey. Otherwise, you cannot take the survey.

Example of Electronic HIPAA Form

CONFIDENTIAL HEALTH CARE INFORMATION (HIPAA)

Authorization to Use or Disclose Health Information

Health information is sensitive information related to a person's medical condition. Because only individuals who have not been medically treated for depression or diagnosed with Attention Deficit Disorder (ADD) will be invited to participate in the study, and because these two conditions are confirmed in the demographics section of the study, a health information release form is required. Therefore, you will need to electronically sign this document before you will be allowed to participate in the study. Otherwise, you will need to withdraw from the study. By signing this health care information form, you give permission to the researcher to use or disclose (release) your health related information as part of the research study. After the data are recorded, the data will be secured in a locked safe for seven years. After seven years, the data will be destroyed. During the seven years, the data will not be disclosed without additional participant consent or unless required by law.

By nature of the study, it will be known to all readers that all of the study's participants have not been medically treated for depression or diagnosed with ADD. Although the results of the research study will be published, your name or identity will not be revealed. The health information provided in the research study will be used by the researcher as a way to control extraneous variables. This information may be confirmed by members of the dissertation committee.

The researcher is required by law to protect your health related information. By electronically signing this document, you authorize the researcher to use and/or disclose your health related information for this research. Those individuals who receive your health related information may not be required by Federal privacy laws to protect the information and they may share it with other people without your permission, if permitted by the laws that govern them.

This authorization has no expiration date. However, you may voluntarily withdraw from the study at any time prior to electronically submitting the data. Once the data are collected, it will no longer be possible to link the data to the signed confidential health care information forms. Please click on the appropriate box below that indicates whether you would like to participate in this study or whether you want to withdraw from this study.

I have read and understand this HIPAA form and

☐ I agree to participate in this study
☐ I do not agree to participate in this study

Example of Electronic Informed Consent Form

INFORMED CONSENT FORM

A Correlational Study of Childhood Religiosity, Childhood Sport Participation, and Sport-Learned Aggression Among African American Female Athletes

Name of University: _____ School Address: _____

Researcher: _____ Phone: _____ E-mail: _____

I am conducting a research study in order to determine the relationships among religiosity, sport participation, and aggression. I would like to invite you to participate in this study. The main purpose of this form is to provide information about the study so that you can make a good decision about whether you want to participate. If you choose to participate, please sign in the space at the end of this form.

I. Background

This study is being conducted in order to assess relationships among variables. The variables include childhood religiosity, childhood sport participation, and aggression. However, it is not necessary that you have played childhood sports. Only African Americans females are being surveyed. You must be from 21 to 40 years of age. You must not have been medically treated for depression. You must not have been diagnosed with Attention Deficit Disorder (ADD). Please read the following information before you make your decision.

II. Purpose

The purpose of this study is to determine the relationships among childhood religiosity, childhood sport participation, and sport-learned aggression. However, other variables may affect the study. Some of them will be controlled by design. Others will be assessed in the demographics part of the survey.

III. Participation

About 500 females have been invited to participate in this study. You have been selected because you represent the study's population. You are an African American female. You are 21 to 40 years of age. You have not been medically treated for depression. You have not been diagnosed with ADD.

Participation is voluntary. You do not have to participate in this study. Nothing will happen to you if you do not want to participate in this study. If you have any questions involving this study, you may call the researcher at xxx-xxx-xxxx.

IV. Procedures

The study will take a total of about 20 minutes to complete. You will mark your answers by clicking on the best response. You will then submit the completed survey online to Zoomerang.

V. Reason for Participation

You have been asked to participate in this study in order to provide data. The data will be used to gain insight on the relationships among variables. The research cannot be performed without data. Your participation provides the needed data.

VI. Research

This study is important in the human services and public safety fields. The study may provide public officials with data that is currently unavailable to them.

VII. Confidentiality

Your personal information is confidential. It will not be disclosed to persons outside of the study without your permission, unless required by law. After the data are recorded, the data will be stored in a locked safe for seven years. After seven years, the data will be destroyed. Furthermore, your name will not be recorded.

The results of the study will be published. However, your name will not be revealed. Completed surveys will only be accessible to the researcher.

All persons involved with this study will honor this agreement. The Institutional Review Board (IRB) will be allowed to inspect sections of the research records related to the study. Members of the IRB or the Human Research Protection Office (HRPO) can answer your questions and concerns about your rights as a research participant. They can be contacted at xxx-xxx-xxxx.

VIII. Risks
No study is completely risk-free. Answering questions about yourself may lead to old memories that generate undesired feelings. However, there is no collaboration or competition in this study and you may withdraw from the study at any time without consequence. The researcher does not anticipate that you will be harmed by participating in this study.

IX. Compensation for Illness or Injury
As a participant, you are not waiving any of your legal rights. However, no funds have been set aside to help you in the event of harm. If you have any questions, you may call the HRPO at xxx-xxx-xxxx.

X. Benefits & Costs
As you are aware, you may receive points, which are of nominal value, from Zoomerang. However, the researcher will not give you anything to participate in this study.

The information from the study may be useful to other people. The only cost to you will be a few moments of your time.

XI. Ownership of Data
The researcher will own the data. This will limit access to the data.

XII. Freedom to Question

You may call the researcher at any time during the study.

XIII. Freedom to Withdraw

Your participation in this study is voluntary. You are free to stop participating in the study at any time without any cost. You do not have to submit any data. However, once data are submitted, it will be too late to withdraw from the study.

XIV. If New Information Becomes Available

The researcher will contact you if he learns about new information that could change your decision about participating in this study.

XV. Voluntary Consent

By signing this form, you are saying that you have read this form. You are saying that you understand the risks and benefits of this study. You are also saying that you know what you are being asked to do. The researcher will be happy to answer any questions you have about the study. If you have any questions, please feel free to call the researcher at xxx-xxx-xxxx.

If you have questions about your rights as a research participant, you may call the HRPO. This is also true if you have any concerns about the research process, the researcher, or experience any unexpected problems with the study. Your identity, questions, and concerns will be kept confidential.

By clicking on the link below, you are saying that you have read this information. You are also saying that you understand what you are being asked to do.

If you click on the following link that indicates *you agree to participate in the study*, your consent as a willing participant will be implied. Otherwise, if you click on the link that indicates *you do not agree to participate in the study*, you will exit the study.

Please print a copy of this consent form for your records.

Choose and click on a link below.

I have read and understand this informed consent form and

- ☐ I agree to participate in the study
- ☐ I do not agree to participate in this study

Research Site(s) Approval

The following institution has granted the researcher access to their participants and/or facilities:

Name: Zoomerang
Approval Date: October 17, 2014
Approval Authorization: 382-7777

IRB Approval

This consent is not valid without the approval information below.

This research has been approved by xxxx University's Institutional Review Board. Approval number: _____; Effective dates: From: _____ to _____. (*This information will be supplied by xxxx University's IRB Office upon the approval of the IRB application.*)

REFERENCES

Balian, E. (1988). *How to design, analyze, and write doctoral or master's research* (2nd ed.). New York, NY: University Press of America.

Berg, B. (2007). *Qualitative research methods for the social sciences* (6th ed.). Boston, MA: Pearson Education, Inc.

Champion, D. (2006). *Research methods for criminal justice and criminology* (3rd ed.). Upper Saddle River, NJ: Pearson Merrill Prentice Hall.

Creswell, J. (2009). *Research design: Qualitative, quantitative, and mixed methods approaches* (3rd ed.). Los Angeles, CA: Sage Publications.

Davis, W.L. (2014). *Religiosity, sports, and learned aggression for Black female athletes.* Saarbrücken, Germany: Scholars.

Hatch, J. (2002). *Doing qualitative research in education settings.* Albany, NY: State University of New York Press.

Neuman, W. (2006). *Social research methods: Qualitative and quantitative approaches* (6th ed.). Boston, MA: Pearson Education, Inc.

Post, M. (2008). *Impact of internal and external factors on working women's successful completion of online college level courses* (Doctoral dissertation). Retrieved from Dissertation Abstracts International-A. (AAT #3316346)

Seale, C., Gobo, G., Gubrium, J., and Silverman, D. (2004). Introduction: Inside qualitative research. In C. Seale, G. Gobo,

J. Gubrium, and D. Silverman (Eds.), *Qualitative research practice* (p. 1-12). Thousand Oaks, CA: Sage Publications.

Zimmerman, J.F. (1997). The Belmont report: An ethical framework for protecting research subjects. *The Monitor.*

CHAPTER 3. RESEARCH PREPARATION

HOW TO SUMMARIZE THE LITERATURE

To be useful, the summary of an academic peer-reviewed study must provide certain intelligence. Remember, the writer is trying to persuade the reader to agree with a particular argument. At a minimum, the researcher should indicate the purpose of the study being reviewed, who were studied, how the data were collected, how the data were analyzed, the findings, and the limitations of the study. For example, a study conducted on white elderly men in Africa may not necessarily be applicable for black female juveniles in the U.S. Do not withhold information from the readers. Provide the readers with enough information so that they may make their own educated decisions. Withholding information may indicate bias or incompetence, which may negatively impact the trustworthiness of the researcher. The credibility of an argument is only as good as its references.

Examples of How to Summarize Academic Articles

Choi, Green, and Gilbert

Choi, Green, and Gilbert (2011) conducted an exploratory qualitative study to determine the perceptions of youths on their experiences in the restorative justice process in order to gain the knowledge needed to develop effective restorative justice practices and policies. Two agency-based program coordinators helped recruit participants by inviting potential participants to participate during their first person-to-person meeting at the Victim-offender mediation (VOM) office in a mid-sized Midwestern city in the U.S. The participants included crime victims, youths who committed crimes and their families, and service providers. The researchers conducted semi-structured interviews of 37 participants in the VOM program and engaged in prolonged observations of the processes for 1-year. Because there is no generally accepted guideline for data analysis and display in qualitative studies, the researchers engaged in constant comparison for data analysis. The researchers read the interview transcripts several times, and by using ATLAS.ti, a software for qualitative data analysis, they unitized all interview transcripts and field notes. After assigning a code to each unit, they conducted a systematic comparison between and within cases, and between and among various perspectives. Subsequently, categories, sub-categories, and themes were identified. The findings indicate that when juvenile delinquents meet their victims through VOM, the youths come to realize the full consequences of their actions by being able to personalize their victims and their victimized experiences.

The Choi et al. (2011) study does have several limitations. First, the study was qualitative in nature and it failed to provide quantitative relationships among the variables. In addition, because the participants were youth offenders who had their families present, their responses may have been influenced by their environment. Finally, because the study involved juvenile offenders, who may be more impressionable, the results may not necessarily apply to adult offenders.

Rudibaugh

Rudibaugh (2015) conducted an ethnography study to understand the culture of a work college in the Appalachian Mountains as experienced by members and partners of the campus community. The researcher, along with two college employees, recruited 12 students and 11 faculty and staff employees to participate in the study. Data were collected via interviews, focus groups, and site observations in the summer months of 2014. Interviews were transcribed and the researcher employed several coding techniques to assess the data: Attribute Coding (determining demographics), Structural Coding (looking for noteworthy similarities and differences for each question across the group), Values Coding (looking for values, attitudes, and beliefs of the participants as they relate to the questions), Code Landscaping (looking at which words appear the most often in the text), and Magnitude Coding (looking to see how codes appear in the text). The findings indicate that three primary themes exist at the college: a) blue collar values of work ethic, b) family environment and cultural congruence, and c) regional and institutional challenges.

The Rudibaugh (2015) study does have several limitations. First, qualitative studies do not allow the researcher to identify cause–and–effect relationships (Leedy, & Ormrod, 2016). In other words, the study failed to provide patterns of relationships through numerical representations (Champion, 2006). In addition, because the sample was convenient, purposive, and non-random, there is a possibility that the participants who chose to participate may be different in meaningful ways from those individuals who chose not to participate. As a result, the findings cannot be generalized to other population groups that do not match the sample's characteristics. Indeed, all of the participants attended one particular work college in the Appalachian Mountains. Thus, the sample may not necessarily represent students at other colleges.

Odegard & Vereen

Odegard and Vereen (2010) conducted a grounded theory qualitative research study to examine the experiences and processes of counselor educators for integrating social justice into their pedagogy across their training curriculum. A grounded theory study begins by understanding the subjective experiences of the participants and then applies inductive reasoning to extract theoretical statements from among the interplay of the subjective experiences. The researchers attempted to elicit individual and collective meanings from the participants.

Odegard and Vereen (2010) used an electronic mailing list to recruit participants from both the Counselors for Social Justice and the Counselor Education and Supervision Network. The researchers recruited four counselor educators who self-identified as integrating social justice into their pedagogy across their curricula: 1) a Caucasian heterosexual male, 40-49 years of age, and assistant professor from the northwest region of the U.S.; 2) a Caucasian heterosexual male, greater than 60 years of age, spiritual, and chair in the far western part of the U.S.; 3) a multiethnic bisexual female, 40-49 years of age, and assistant professor from the northwest region of the U.S.; and 4) a Caucasian, Hispanic, and Native American male, 40-49 years of age, a Unitarian Universalist, and assistant professor from the Midwestern region of the U.S.

Odegard and Vereen (2010) collected data via two rounds of interviews, member checks between the interviews, and focus groups. The first interview lasted about 45 minutes and the goal was to understand the meaning behind each participant's responses and to determine the similarities among the participants' responses. After the interviews, Odegard met with an inquiry auditor, Vereen, who questioned the research findings throughout the data analysis process in order to determine the accuracy of the initial concepts. Each participant was then mailed a transcript of his or her particular interview to confirm the validity of the interview. After the member checking process, a second round of interviews took place to further cultivate the developing grounded theory. Following the second interview, each participant was again mailed a transcript of his or her particular interview to confirm the validity of the interview. Finally, the researchers conducted a 45 minute focus group interview via telephone. After the interview, each participant was sent a conceptual map of the grounded theory and asked about his or her perceptions of the theory.

All interviews were recorded, transcribed, and reviewed for accuracy (Odegard & Vereen, 2010). Odegard served as the primary coder and, in order to enhance credibility, Vereen served as the inquiry auditor. The coding procedures included open coding, axial coding, and selective coding. Open coding develops concepts by exposing the ideas, thoughts, and meanings contained within the text. Axial coding reconstructs the data that are fractured during the open coding by relating categories to subcategories. Selective coding creates a core category by combining and refining categories around a central concept. The findings indicate that the grounded theory of counselor educators who integrate social justice into their pedagogy was best represented by the concepts of a) facilitating a paradigm shift, b) increasing awareness, and c) navigating challenges.

The Odegard and Vereen (2010) study does have several limitations. First, only participants from CACREP-accredited programs were selected. Perhaps these participants are different in a meaningful way from individuals who are not associated with CACREP-accredited programs. Second, the focus group interviews were conducted via telephone. Thus, important nonverbal communication remains unexplored. Third, because of the extended time between the interviews and the review of the transcripts, some of the participants have reported memory lapses, which may have impacted the validity of the data. Finally, the small sample size associated with the study may prevent the findings from being generalized to a larger population.

ANNOTATED BIBLIOGRAPHY

Annotated Bibliography 1 - Marijuana

All four sources listed below are credible, as evidenced by the credentials of the authors. However, the sources are only moderately credible because they are textbooks and brochures; they are not academic, peer-reviewed research studies. All sources listed below examine marijuana or deviance, which relate to the topic of interest.

Earleywine, M. (2002). *Understanding marijuana: A new look at the scientific evidence.* **New York: Oxford University Press.**

The author, who is the Director of Clinical Training in Psychology at the University of Southern California and a leading researcher in psychology and addiction, conducted a review of research on marijuana and provides a balanced view of the biological, psychological, and social impact of marijuana use (Earleywine, 2002). Through academic rigor, the author traces the medical and political debates and separates science from opinions. By providing objective information, the author provides an overall view of the current demand for marijuana. The data indicate that the War on Drugs is a failure. At a minimum, a policy change is required.

Gahlinger, P. (2004). *Illegal drugs: A complete guide to their history, chemistry, use, and abuse.* **New York, NY: Plume.**

The author, a physician and certified substance abuse medical review officer, has studied the effects of drugs in various settings (Gahlinger, 2004). Because the author believes that the War on Drugs has been a failure and that the best solution to the drug problem begins with education, he has written this book to provide objective information. With the input from Drug Enforcement Agency (DEA) officers, substance abuse counselors, the Department of Pharmacology and Family and Preventative Medicine, and drug users, the author collected data and has found that there are two opposing sides to the drug debate. One side believes that marijuana is a health issue and should be controlled by the government, and the other side believes that marijuana is a safe recreational drug that should not controlled by the government. The data provided by the author contributes to the understanding of marijuana's history, its chemical properties and effects, its medical uses, its recreational abuses, its associated health problems, and its impact on America's cultural and economic systems. The author also indicates how the media use their power to influence marijuana policies.

Indiana State Police (1997). [Brochure]. *Marijuana: Get straight on the facts.* **New Orleans, LA: Syndistar, Inc.**

The author, who is the leading law enforcement agency in the State of Indiana, has the legal authority and responsibility to enforce marijuana laws (Indiana State Police, 1997). This agency states that it will solve problems, reduce crime, and promote public safety by openly communicating with the public and other governmental agencies. Because marijuana possession and consumption is presently illegal in Indiana, the author has created a brochure in which to educate people on the consequences of possessing and consuming marijuana. The author clearly states that marijuana laws will be enforced.

Liska, A. and Messner, S. (1999). *Perspectives on crime and deviance* **(3rd ed.). Upper Saddle River, NJ: Prentice Hall.**

Liska was a professor at the University of Albany, State University of New York and was considered an expert in the field of criminology and deviance and was named a Fellow of the American Society of Criminology (Liska & Messner, 1999). With Messner, who is currently a Distinguished Teaching Professor at that same university, they present case studies, historic and cotemporary illustrations, and statistics in order to apply theories to crime and deviance. Their focus is on the understanding of research strategies and how they can test theories involving deviance. In this case, the authors provide an explanation as to why marijuana is classified as contraband. What makes deviance a crime is that there are a small group of people in power who arbitrarily define it that way in order to protect their own self-interests. This puts the law on their side and creates conflict.

Annotated Bibliography 2 - Situational Crime Prevention

All four sources listed below are credible, as evidenced by the credentials of the authors. The sources are highly credible because they are academic, peer-reviewed research studies. All sources listed below examine situational crime prevention (SCP) measures, which relate to the topic of interest.

LaVigne, N. (1996). Safe transport: Security by design on the Washington metro. *Crime Prevention Studies*, 6, 163-197.

Dr. Nancy LaVigne received her doctorate degree in educational psychology from McGill University in Montreal and is a professor at the University of Delaware (LaVigne, 1996). She has numerous publications in peer-reviewed journals, book chapters, and technical reports. In this study, LaVigne investigates the implementation of Situational Crime Prevention (SCP) measures in the Washington, D.C. Metro subway system using quantitative techniques.

After implementing SCP measures in the Metro subway system, crime data that are reported to the police were collected (LaVigne, 1996). Analysis of variance (ANOVA) and F-tests were then used to compare this subway system to the subway systems in Chicago, Boston, and Atlanta, which do not employ SCP measures. The findings ($F = 8.45$, $p = 0.001$) indicate that the Metro subway system's mean rate of crime is significantly lower than the other three subway systems. Unlike the other three subway systems, the Metro subway system is designed so that the customer waiting area is free of obstructions and is highly visible, the system utilizes closed circuit televisions, the area is well lit and maintained, and the laws are stringently enforced. As a result, the Metro subway system is believed to be one of the safest subway systems in the country.

Beavon, D., Brantingham, P., and Brantingham, P. (1994). The influence of street networks on the patterning of property offenses. *Crime Prevention Studies,* **2, 115–148.**

Daniel Beavon, Director of Strategic Research and Analysis Directorate of Indian and Northern Affairs Canada, Patricia Brantingham, a mathematician and Director of the Institute of Canadian Urban Research Studies, and Paul Brantingham, a lawyer and past Director of Special Reviews at the Public Service Commission of Canada, examine the relationships between accessibility of street networks, property crime, and concentration of potential victims (Newhouse, Voyager, & Beavon, 2005). A quantitative research study was conducted in two towns over a one-year time period where the official crime rate as reported to the police was examined in various street segments (Beavon, Brantingham, & Brantingham, 1994). In evaluating the relationship between street accessibility and breaking and entering, one-way ANOVA and Pearson Correlation statistical techniques were employed.

The findings ($F_{4,1570}$ = 9.735, p = 0.0000; r = 0.97039, R^2 = 0.94149, p = 0.00306) indicate that the crime rate is significantly greater on streets that are more accessible to the public and that are used more often (Beavon et al., 1994). Thus, criminal opportunities vary depending upon the environment in which one lives. In these cases, potential offenders have the opportunity to search for their targets in these highly traveled areas, and opportunities seem to dominate the pattern of criminal behaviors.

Atlas, R., and LeBlanc, W. (1994). The impact on crime of street closures and barricades: A Florida case study. *Security Journal,* **140–145.**

Dr. Robert Atlas, a national security trainer and America's only expert architect/criminologist, and Dr. William LeBlanc, who earned his doctorate degree in experimental psychology and who specializes in research design and analysis of data, study the implementation of SCP measures to the traffic flow in a local neighborhood by using barricades (Atlas & LeBlanc, 1994; "Expert witness", 2008). Reported crime data from the City of Miami Shores, Metro Dade County, and the City of Miami were examined before and after the implementation of barricades in the City of Miami Shores. However, because changes in the crime rates within the communities were the subject of interest, statistical comparisons were only performed within each municipality and not between the municipalities.

Using a multiple range test (MRT) to compare the pre-barricade and post-barricade reported crime data, the findings indicate that burglaries, larcenies, and auto thefts had significantly decreased in Miami Shores over a 7-year time period (Atlas & LeBlanc, 1994). Thus, by implementing SCP measures, such as by changing street designs and by closing roads, vehicular traffic can be controlled. By controlling vehicular traffic in a particular area, crime in that area can be reduced. However, the findings also indicate that crime in the neighboring areas had increased during this same time period, possibly the result of crime displacement.

Knutsson, J. (1996). Restoring public order in a city park. *Crime Prevention Studies*, 7, 133-151.

Johannes Knutsson, a 2004 Herman Goldstein Award finalist, is a professor of police research at the Norwegian Police University College in Norway and has published several studies on crime prevention measures (UCL Jill Dando Institute of Crime Science, 2005). In this research study, Knutsson (1996) studied the implementation of SCP measures in a city park, which was considered a drug dealing hot spot. Data were collected by surveying local residents, by interviewing local businesses and park drug offenders, and by performing site observations.

Using chi-square analysis, the findings (Chi Sq. = 101.70, d.f.= 4, $p < 0.0001$) indicate that SCP measures reduced the perceived level of criminal activity in the area (Knutsson, 1996). Thus, by controlling foot traffic in the park and by making the area more visible to other people, crime in the area was reduced. However, the findings also suggest that some crime displacement did occur.

ANNOTATED OUTLINE

Police & Gratuities

I.   Introduction to the Problem: Police officers accepting gratuities is not uncommon (Hess & Wrobleski, 1997). Because police officers have discretionary powers, and because their attitudes may be influenced by gratuities, accepting gratuities may create a problem if they impact the performance of their duties.

II. Purpose of the Study: The purpose of this study is to understand how police officers perceive their accepting of gratuities impacts public relations and job performance. Police officers accepting gratuities may be good or bad (Coleman, 2004; Prenzler & Mackay, 1995; Pozo, 2005; Ruiz & Bono, 2004).
     A. Pros of Police Officers Accepting Gratuities
     B. Cons of Police Officers Accepting Gratuities

III. Research Questions: In order to understand the reality of police officers accepting gratuities as perceived by police officers, two qualitative research questions have been developed (Adams, 1999).
     A. How do State Police officers describe their perceptions that accepting gratuities may affect their enforcement of traffic laws and the quality of public services that they provide?
     B. What do State Police officers believe the public thinks about them accepting gratuities?

IV. Theoretical Framework: Officers accept gratuities because they learn from other officers that the benefits of accepting gratuities are greater than the associated costs (Siegel, 2003).
     A. Rational Choice Theory
     B. Social Learning Theory

V.   Definition of Terms: Definition of terms may be inconsistent among different individuals (Coleman, 2004; Prenzler & Mackay, 1995). Thus, these terms need to be clarified so that a common understanding of the problem is developed.
   A. Gratuities
   B. Discretionary Decisions
   C. Public Service

VI. Assumptions and Limitations: It is assumed that the police officers are truthful in their disclosures and that they can detect and interpret the feelings of other people. Limitations include limited applications of the findings to other populations (Leedy & Ormrod, 2016).
   A. Assumptions
   B. Limitations

VII. Literature Review: The literature review will investigate 1) the influence of gratuities on police officers, 2) the attitude of police officers compared to criminal justice students, 3) whether an ethics course is effective in modifying behaviors, 4) the attitude of the general public, 5) the prevalence of police officers accepting gratuities, and 6) whether officers are willing to self-police themselves in changing their ways (Ivkovic, 2004; Kirchgraber, 2004; Lord & Bjerregaard, 2003; MacIntyre & Prenzler, 1999; Prenzler & Mackay, 1995; Trautman, 2001).
   A. Police Officers' Attitudes
   B. Police Officers versus Criminal Justice Students
   C. Criminal Justice Ethics Course
   D. General Public Perceptions
   E. Prevalence of Accepting Gratuities
   F. Code of Silence

VIII. Methodology: The research design will employ in-depth, personal, semi-structured interviews based on a phenomenological approach. This method attempts to understand the perceptions of police officers and how these perceptions impact discretionary decisions (Hatch, 2002; Leedy & Ormrod, 2016). The sampling will be purposive, the sample size will be small (i.e., 12 participants), the instrument will consist of several open-ended questions, data will be collected via interviews and transcribed verbatim, and the data will be context analyzed (Berg, 2007; Creswell, 2003).

   A. Research design
   B. Sampling
   C. Instruments
   D. Data Collection Procedures
   E. Data Analysis Procedures

IX. Significance of the Study: This study is significant because all U.S. residents are under some sort of police authority. Because proper police service requires good police-community relations and fair treatment of all persons, it is important to know if gratuities interfere with police performance (Carter, 2002). The results may provide an assessment of police management's traditional approach to managing gratuities and may indicate the need for future policy changes.

   A. Findings
   B. Conclusions
   C. Recommendations

<u>TENTATIVE BUDGET</u>

Example of a Qualitative Tentative Budget

It is important to know if the study is financially feasible. In addition, it is important to know that a third party is not influencing the researcher's interpretation of the study's findings via its financial support. With a sample size of 12 participants and an average interview time of 3 hours, the estimated total budget is about $5,200. The $5,200 can be broken down as follows: $720 for data collector, $240 for the participant incentive fee, $1,440 for the transcription fee, $2,000 for the coding transcription fee, $500 for the transportation fee, $200 for data analysis software, and $100 for supplies.

<u>Tentative Budget (Qualitative Study of 12 participants)</u>

Salaries = $20/hr

Time to interview: 12 interviews x 3 hrs each = 36 hours

Data collection (36 hrs x $20/hr) =	$720
Participant incentive (12 participants x $20/participant) =	$240
Transcription (72 hours x $20/hr) =	$1,440
Coding transcription fee (100 hrs x $20/hr) =	$2,000
Transportation fee (200 miles to collect all data) =	$500
Cost of data analysis software =	$200
<u>Supplies =</u>	<u>$100</u>
Total Budget =	$5,200

It is important to forecast what a study will cost. If the total expected cost is too high, then management may not approve the study. Although the itemized costs may not be exact, they do provide a general figure of expected expenses, which may be important for budgeting purposes. Because it may take a long time to collect in-depth information, a small increase in the sample size can significantly increase the cost of a qualitative study. Furthermore, because it may take a long time to collect data in a qualitative study, individuals may need to be offered a financial incentive to motivate them to participate. In short, a qualitative study can obtain very detailed information, but at a very high cost per participant.

<u>DISCUSSION QUESTIONS/EXERCISES</u>

1) From your own community, provide some specific examples of negative perceptions between the police and community members that have caused or may cause poor police-community relations. Suggest ways to modify these negative perceptions.

2) What are the main complaints of minorities against the police? Discuss why the view of minorities toward the police may be different than that of Caucasians. Describe how a resident's experience with the police may shape the resident's image of all officers. What is the main complaint of police officers?

3) Discuss the reasons behind the Benton Harbor (MI) riot. You are a police chief. Discuss ways that you can prevent future riots.

4) A controversial issue is related to how a police officer's performance review is determined. Discuss the pros and cons for the traditional quantitative evaluation of performance (i.e.., quotas). Discuss how a qualitative evaluation method can be employed.

5) Perform a literature review on a criminal justice topic and summarize three scholarly, peer-reviewed research studies. When you summarize each study, answer the following questions. 1) What was the purpose of the study? 2) Who were studied? 3) How were data collected? 4) What data analysis technique was used? 5) What were the findings? 6) What were the limitations of the study?

6) Researchers are required to use ethical procedures when performing studies. Discuss the ethical procedures.

7) The Institutional Review Board (IRB) is required to approve all university affiliated studies. Why did the IRB come about? What should be presented on an **informed consent form** before any research is conducted? Why?

<u>TEAM ASSUMPTIONS – CLASS ACTIVITY</u>

Individuals make assumptions about other people. We draw conclusions about other people based on experiences, rumors, and personal filters. Without knowing it, these assumptions are often displayed by how we communicate with one another.

<u>Class Activity</u>

1) Write words on 3" x 5" cards that describe human qualities/ behaviors (e.g., clown, imbecile, genius, happy, grumpy, cry baby, lazy, feminist, etc.).

2) Have group members sit at a table and tape the unique word on a stick above and behind each individual. Do not let the individual see the word that will represent that particular person. Each individual will see every word that describes all the other individuals. The only word that each person cannot see will be the one that describes himself/herself.

3) Have the group play a game of cards.

4) Without saying the word behind each person, individuals are to treat all other individuals according to the word that describes each person. Assumptions will be made about one another based on the description written on each person's card.

5) After playing for a while, each participant will be asked to guess what word is listed on the card behind him/her.

6) The rest of the class will take notes on what they observe.

ASSESSING QUALITATIVE INFORMATION

Value of Information

The value of information is relative. What is considered important information to some individuals may be considered less important to other individuals. Police officers need to understand that certain individuals will seek out particular information. Police officers will be more effective if they understand what information certain people value.

Read the following paragraph and highlight important information.

A man entered a home. There were surveillance cameras all about the home. Inside the home, there was a strong odor of mold in the air. There was a big flat-screen TV and a laptop in the living room. In the kitchen was a backed-up sink and the pipe was leaking. Near the sink were a woman's diamond ring and a gold watch. There was a desk in a study in which there was a wad of cash; there was also a safe in one of the closets. In one of the bedrooms was the sound of someone snoring; there was also some water dripping from the bedroom's ceiling. A car then pulled into the driveway.

Now, read the following paragraph and highlight important information from a thief's point of view. Assume the man who entered the home was the thief.

A man entered a home. There were surveillance cameras all about the home. Inside the home, there was a strong odor of mold in the air. There was a big flat-screen TV and a laptop in the living room. In the kitchen was a backed-up sink and the pipe was leaking. Near the sink were a woman's diamond ring and a gold watch. There was a desk in a study in which there was a wad of cash; there was also a safe in one of the closets. In one of the bedrooms was the sound of someone snoring; there was also some water dripping from the bedroom's ceiling. A car then pulled into the driveway.

Now, read the following paragraph and highlight important information from a potential home buyer's point of view. Assume the man who entered the home was the potential home buyer.

A man entered a home. There were surveillance cameras all about the home. Inside the home, there was a strong odor of mold in the air. There was a big flat-screen TV and a laptop in the living room. In the kitchen was a backed-up sink and the pipe was leaking. Near the sink were a woman's diamond ring and a gold watch. There was a desk in a study in which there was a wad of cash; there was also a safe in one of the closets. In one of the bedrooms was the sound of someone snoring; there was also some water dripping from the bedroom's ceiling. A car then pulled into the driveway.

Summary

A thief and potential home buyer will value the same information differently. What is important to the thief may not be important to the potential home buyer. Likewise, what is important to the potential home buyer may not be important to the thief.

How the Exercise applies to Law Enforcement

Police officers cannot effectively serve the community if the officers do not understand the community. Because laws in the U.S. are typically based on men's perspective, the laws are inherently biased; females may not necessarily agree with those laws. From the feminist perspective, women face issues that may appear obscure to men (Hatch, 2002). For females to more effectively influence public policies, they must be equally represented within the state and federal governments. By controlling 50% of the power, females may better influence laws and public policies. Female officers have essential knowledge and experience needed to help solve local community issues.

Figure 2. T. Pavlick, a South Carolina Female Law Enforcer

REFERENCES

Adams, W. (1999). The interpermeation of self and world: Empirical research, existential phenomenology, and transpersonal psychology. *Journal of Phenomenological Psychology*, 30(2), 39-65.

Atlas, R., and LeBlanc, W. (1994). The impact on crime of street closures and barricades: A Florida case study. *Security Journal*, 140-145.

Beavon, D., Brantingham, P., and Brantingham, P. (1994). The influence of street networks on the patterning of property offenses. *Crime Prevention Studies*, *2*, 115-148.

Berg, B. (2007). *Qualitative research methods for the social sciences* (6ᵗʰ ed.). Boston, MA: Pearson Education, Inc.

Carter, D. (2002). *Issues in police-community relations: Taken from The Police and the community* (7ᵗʰ ed.). Boston, MA: Pearson Custom Publishing.

Champion, D. (2006). *Research methods for criminal justice and criminology* (3ʳᵈ ed.). Upper Saddle River, NJ: Pearson Merrill Prentice Hall.

Choi, J.J., Green, D.L., & Gilbert, M.J. (2011). Putting a human face of crimes: A qualitative study on restorative justice processes for youths. *Child and Adolescent Social Work Journal*, *28*(5), 335-355. doi: 10.1007/s10560-011-0238-9.

Coleman, S. (2004). When police should say "no!" to gratuities. *Criminal Justice Ethics*, *23*(1), 33-44.

Creswell, J. (2003). *Research design: Qualitative, quantitative, and mixed methods approaches* (2nd ed.). Thousand Oaks, CA: Sage Publications.

Earleywine, M. (2002). *Understanding marijuana: A new look at the scientific evidence.* New York: Oxford University Press.

Expert witness directory jurispro: Dr. Randall I. Atlas (2008). Retrieved from http://www.jurispro.com/RandallAtlas

Gahlinger, P. (2004). *Illegal drugs: A complete guide to their history, chemistry, use, and abuse.* New York, NY: Plume.

Hatch, J. (2002). *Doing qualitative research in education settings.* Albany, NY: State University of New York Press.

Hess, K., and Wrobleski, H. (1997). *Police operations: Theory and practice* (2nd ed.). St. Paul, MN: West publishing Company.

Indiana State Police (1997). [Brochure]. *Marijuana: Get straight on the facts.* New Orleans, LA: Syndistar, Inc.

Ivkovic, S. (2004). Evaluating the seriousness of police misconduct: A cross-cultural comparison of police officer and citizen views. *International Criminal Justice Review, 14,* 25-48.

Kirchgraber, T. (2004, November 1). When policy and practice collide: The mixed message on gratuities. *Sheriff.*

Knutsson, J. (1996). Restoring public order in a city park. *Crime Prevention Studies, 7,* 133-151.

LaVigne, N. (1996). Safe transport: Security by design on the Washington metro. *Crime Prevention Studies, 6,* 163-197.

Leedy, P., and Ormrod, J. (2016). *Practical research: Planning and design* (11th ed.). Boston, MA: Pearson.

Liska, A. and Messner, S. (1999). *Perspectives on Crime and Deviance* (3rd ed.). Upper Saddle River, NJ: Prentice Hall.

Lord, V., and Bjerregaard, B. (2003). Ethics courses: Their impact on the values and ethical decisions on criminal justice students. *Journal of Criminal Justice Management, 14*(2), 191-211.

MacIntyre, S., and Prenzler, T. (1999). The influence of gratuities and personal relationships on police use of discretion. *Policing and Society, 9*(2), 181-201.

Newhouse, D., Voyager, C., and Beavon, D. (2005). Hidden in plain sight: Contributions of Aboriginal peoples to Canadian identity and culture, volume 1 (Eds.). *University of Toronto Press Inc.*

Odegard, M.A., & Vereen, L.G. (2010). A grounded theory of counselor educators integrating social justice into their pedagogy. *Counselor Education & Supervision, 50*, 130-149.

Pozo, B. (2005). One dogma of police ethics: Gratuities and the "democratic ethos" of policing. *Criminal Justice Ethics, 24*(2), 25-46.

Prenzler, T., and Mackay, P. (1995). Police gratuities: What the public think. *Criminal Justice Ethics, 14*(1), 15-25.

Rudibaugh, L.M. (2015). Helping the way we are needed: Ethnography of an Appalachian work college. *Dissertations & Theses.* (UMI No. 3707735).

Ruiz, J., and Bono, C. (2004). At what price a "freebie'? The real cost of police gratuities. *Criminal Justice Ethics, 23*(1), 44-54.

Siegel, L. (2003). *Criminology* (8th ed.). Belmont, CA: Thomson Wadsworth.

Trautman, N. (2001, March 1). The code of silence... now we know the truth. *Sheriff.*

UCL Jill Dando Institute of Crime Science (2005). Retrieved from the University College London Web site: http://www.jdi.ucl.ac.uk/people/academic/knutsson.php

CHAPTER 4. EXAMPLE OF AN ABRIDGED RESEARCH PROPOSAL

Qualitative Case Study: Police Officers Accepting Gratuities

Abstract

Police officers accepting gratuities is not uncommon. Because police officers have discretionary powers, and because their attitudes may be influenced by accepting gratuities, this may create a problem if this impacts the performance of their duties. Thus, in order to learn more about this poorly understood problem from the police officers' perspective, a qualitative longitudinal case study involving five Indiana State Police cadets will be performed, following the officers for two years after they graduate from the police academy. This study will allow incremental behavioral changes to be measured at specific points in time.

Purpose of the Study

The purpose of this study is to understand how police officers perceive their accepting of gratuities impacts public relations and their job performance.

Qualitative Research Question

In order to understand the nature of police officers accepting gratuities as perceived by police officers, the following qualitative research question has been developed. *How do police officers perceive the accepting of gratuities impacts personal relationships and their discretionary decisions?*

Theoretical Framework: Rational Choice and Social Learning Theories

The rational choice theory, based on Beccaria's classical school of criminology, claims that people freely choose their behaviors (Siegel, 2003). It is believed that people calculate the potential benefits and costs associated with each behavior and then they choose to perform those acts that are profitable.

The social learning theory, as developed by Albert Bandura, combines operant conditioning and cognitive psychology (Siegel, 2003). According to this theory, behaviors can be learned and reinforced through personal rewards and punishments and by observing the rewards and punishments of other people.

Assumptions and Limitations

It is assumed that the police officers are truthful in their disclosures and that they can detect and interpret the feelings of other people. In addition, limitations include limited applications of the findings to other populations (Leedy & Ormrod, 2016).

Literature Review

There are several research studies involving police gratuities. First, an Australian ex post facto quantitative descriptive study measured police officers' attitudes toward accepting gratuities by providing them with various hospitality scenarios (MacIntyre & Prenzler, 1999). The findings indicate that police officers' attitudes may be influenced by accepting gratuities. Second, a cross-cultural quantitative study of police officers and college students indicate that police officers are significantly less tolerant than college students of accepting gratuities (Ivkovic, 2004). Third, a quasi-experiment pretest-posttest study indicates that one college course in ethics is not enough to develop values or behavioral changes in college students (Lord & Bjerregaard,

2003). Fourth, an ex post facto quantitative descriptive study indicates that there is strong community support that favors police officers not accepting gratuities (Prenzler & Mackay, 1995). Fifth, an ex post facto quantitative descriptive study investigates city, county, and state law enforcement agencies in Florida (Kirchgraber, 2004). The findings indicate that police officers do regularly accept gratuities. Finally, a mixed methods ex post facto study was performed examining the code of silence (Trautman, 2001). The findings indicate that the code of silence is common and that police officers do not readily inform management about each other's questionable behaviors, such as accepting gratuities.

Proposal for Research Design

To capture the participants' points of view involving their beliefs, attitudes, and behaviors surrounding the event of accepting gratuities, a qualitative case study is appropriate (Creswell, 2003). In this study, five cadets (i.e., participants) will be assessed while at the police academy before they are sworn police officers and before they are provided gratuities, and then they will be followed for two years after graduation. Interviews will be conducted with each participant once a month and other pertinent information about the topic, including department policies, disciplinary postings, and newspaper articles, will be gathered to supplement and substantiate the interviews.

Methodology

Research Design

Different research designs have different strengths and weaknesses. First, ex post facto quantitative descriptive studies, where data are collected after the fact, are effective in determining the impact of the independent variable (e.g., accepting gratuities) on the dependent variable (e.g., behaviors), but the independent variable cannot be manipulated (Leedy & Ormrod, 2016). Thus, definite conclusions about cause and effect cannot be established. Second, focus group interviews, where individuals who share common traits and experiences interact and provide data beyond what any single participant could provide, are most appropriate for studies that are explanatory in nature (Hatch, 2002). However, a weakness in this technique is that the group consensus may overshadow a particular individual's perspective (Berg, 2007; Hatch). Third, phenomenology, which explores the essence of experience, gains a deeper understanding of an experience and uncovers hidden phenomena (Hatch). However, these studies are based on interviews that may take place long after the fact and may be influenced by forgetfulness and exaggeration. Fourth, unobtrusive ethnography seeks to describe a culture from the local or indigenous people's point of view through participant observation and artifact examination in order "to understand the cultural knowledge that group members use to make sense of the everyday experiences" (Hatch, p. 21). However, the weaknesses in unobtrusive data are 1) the data presents a distorted view of the events and social context, 2) the data are gathered piecemeal, presenting an incomplete picture, and 3) those individuals initially presenting documented records may have done so in a biased fashion. Finally, a case study is a type of qualitative research where in–depth data are collected on a single event, program, or individual bound by time and activity for the purpose of learning more about a poorly understood problem (Creswell, 2003; Hatch; Leedy & Ormrod, 2016). Indeed, a case study, which focuses on few participants, will be most effective in understanding how police officers develop their attitudes about accepting gratuities (Berg, 2007).

There are four advantages in performing case studies (Champion, 2006). First, case studies are flexible and they allow the researcher to collect data in multiple ways, such as by interviewing people and by examining records. Second, this flexibility can be extended to virtually any dimension of the gratuities topic. Third, case studies can be performed in many types of social environments. Finally, a longitudinal case study will allow incremental behavioral changes to be measured at specific points in time.

There are three disadvantages in performing case studies (Champion, 2006). First, case study findings are unique to particular individuals and settings and may not be generalized to other populations. Second, attrition is a concern; participants may simply lose interest and stop participating. Third, findings from individual case studies may not always support theories. Therefore, an accumulation of case studies is important.

Sampling

The sampling will employ a non-probability sampling design based on purposive criterion sampling. Five Indiana State Police cadets will be selected based on who responds first to the study's invitation.

Instrument

The following are five open-ended questions that will allow for narrative style responses. *"What is the police department's position on accepting gratuities?" "What does the public think about you accepting gratuities?" "What are the advantages and disadvantages of accepting gratuities?" "How does a police officer accepting gratuities differ from doctors, politicians, or restaurant employees accepting gratuities (free perks) in their respective trades?"* And, *"How has accepting gratuities created personal relationships with store owners, which have affected your discretionary enforcement of minor violations of the law or the delivering of public services?"*

Data

This qualitative research design will employ in-depth, personal, semi-structured interviews by utilizing a multiple subject longitudinal case study (Champion, 2006). One-hour interviews will be conducted once a month, tape recorded, and transcribed verbatim. Furthermore, department policies, disciplinary postings, and newspaper articles will be gathered to supplement and substantiate the interviews (Berg, 2007).

The data will be context analyzed (Berg, 2007; Creswell, 2003). Content analysis "is a systematic technique for categorizing words into content categories using special coding rules" (Churyk, Lee, & Clinton, 2008, p. 52). Groupings of words will reflect themes, and the evaluation of themes will provide answers to the research question.

Philosophical, Political, and Ethical Issues

There are philosophical, political, and ethical issues when police officers accept gratuities. These issues are important because law and order depend upon residents submitting themselves to the government in order to be governed (Carter, 2002). This requires faith that the officers will be just, but faith is influenced by image. Indeed, if the public becomes dissatisfied with police and breaks the agreement, then chaos will result.

Because proper police service requires good police-community relations and fair treatment of all persons, it is important to know if gratuities interfere with police officer performance (Carter, 2002). Indeed, the results of this study may provide an assessment of police management's traditional approach to managing gratuities and may indicate the need for future policy changes.

The police officer code of ethics does not necessarily disapprove of police officers accepting gratuities (Hess & Wrobleski, 1997). However, the concern is that accepting gratuities may negatively affect a police officer's discretionary decisions. Because accepting gratuities may be good, such as in developing positive social relationships, or bad, such as in leading to corruption, this study is essential in determining which is true.

Strategies to Help Facilitate Study

In order to protect participants, ethical guidelines will be followed throughout the research process. First, the purpose of the study and its benefits will be effectively communicated to the participants (Creswell, 2003). Second, because participation is voluntary, it will be made clear to the participants that they can withdraw from the study at any time without consequence. Third, to help protect anonymity, names will not be attached to the data collection instruments. Fourth, to protect the confidentiality of the data, a Certificate of Confidentiality will be sought (Berg, 2007). Fifth, member checking will be employed to ensure accurate interpretations of the data (Creswell).

REFERENCES

Berg, B. (2007). *Qualitative research methods for the social sciences* (6th ed.). Boston, MA: Pearson Education, Inc.

Carter, D. (2002). *Issues in police-community relations: Taken from The Police and the community* (7th ed.). Boston, MA: Pearson Custom Publishing.

Champion, D. (2006). *Research methods for criminal justice and criminology* (3rd ed.). Upper Saddle River, NJ: Pearson Merrill Prentice Hall.

Churyk, N., Lee, C., and Clinton, D. (2008). Can we detect fraud earlier? *Strategic Finance, 90*(4), 51-54.

Creswell, J. (2003). *Research design: Qualitative, quantitative, and mixed methods approaches* (2nd ed.). Thousand Oaks, CA: Sage Publications.

Hatch, J. (2002). *Doing qualitative research in education settings.* Albany, NY: State University of New York Press.

Hess, K., and Wrobleski, H. (1997). *Police operations: Theory and practice* (2nd ed.). St. Paul, MN: West publishing Company.

Ivkovic, S. (2004). Evaluating the seriousness of police misconduct: A cross-cultural comparison of police officer and citizen views. *International Criminal Justice Review, 14,* 25-48.

Kirchgraber, T. (2004, November 1). When policy and practice collide: The mixed message on gratuities. *Sheriff.* Retrieved from http://www.highbeam.com/doc/1P3-750878951.html

Leedy, P., and Ormrod, J. (2016). *Practical research: Planning and design* (11th ed.). Boston, MA: Pearson.

Lord, V., and Bjerregaard, B. (2003). *Ethics courses: Their impact on the values and ethical decisions on criminal justice students. Journal of Criminal Justice Management, 14(2), 191-211.*

MacIntyre, S., and Prenzler, T. (1999). The influence of gratuities and personal relationships on police use of discretion. *Policing and Society, 9*(2), 181-201.

Prenzler, T., and Mackay, P. (1995). Police gratuities: What the public think. *Criminal Justice Ethics, 14*(1), 15-25.

Siegel, L. (2003). *Criminology* (8th ed.). Belmont, CA: Thomson Wadsworth.

Trautman, N.E. (2001, March 1). The code of silence... now we know the truth. *Sheriff.* Retrieved from http://www.highbeam. com/doc/1P3-69904278.html

PART II

CHAPTER 5. A COMPREHENSIVE QUALITATIVE RESEARCH STUDY

PERCEPTIONS AND ATTITUDES OF PARTNER ABUSE AMONG AFRICAN AMERICANS

Abstract

The purpose of this study was to evaluate the perceptions and attitudes of partner abuse among African Americans. Domestic violence among intimate partners is one of the most relevant topics to our culture in the United States today. Research into the African American community about the perceptions and attitudes of domestic violence will bring forth a level of consciousness as to how culture affects domestic violence. The perceptions and attitudes among African Americans toward domestic violence were examined by looking at the level of income in the home, the level of education completed, as well as a relationship with someone who has been or is still in a domestic violence relationship. The study utilized a correlational survey design using a cross-sectional survey technique comprised of 43 African American business leaders working in areas of the Panhandle of Florida, such as Panama City and Pensacola. One of the main hypothesis states that education plays a significant role in the perceptions and attitudes of African American business leaders toward partner abuse; according to the results, formal education was not one of the factors that contribute to domestic violence among African American business leaders in the Panhandle of Florida. Results showed that there was not a significant difference for married and unmarried participants regarding the attitude and perception of partner abuse. However, the results did show that among African American businessmen and business women, there was a significant difference for participants of various occupations regarding the attitude and perception of partner abuse.

Table of Contents

List of Tables

List of Figures

CHAPTER 1. INTRODUCTION

Domestic violence among intimate partners is one of the most relevant topics to our culture in the United States today. It is especially relevant to those individuals who are faced with it daily. Continued research for domestic violence is urgent in our society because this issue can become a fatal matter. If solutions are not found and managed, more men and women will continue to suffer as victims. Domestic violence is an issue that is very real and serious. Lutenbacher, Cohen, and Mitzel (2003) agreed that this issue is serious; they also indicate that domestic violence is becoming a public health concern. Women are ten times more likely to be victims of domestic violence than men, with the highest prevalence of women as victims of intimate partners. Men are also victims of domestic violence; however, according to Lutenbacher, Cohen, and Mitzel (2003) in their research, they deduced that the more prevalent number was among women.

Caracci (2003) adds to Lutenbacher, Cohen, and Mitzel (2003) the same sentiment by stating that intimate violence against women stretches across social boundaries. He agrees that due to the serious repercussions women face because of intimate violence, this issue has become a priority in the public health arena. Many women in the U.S. live in constant fear.

Unfortunately, the fear many of these women experience is not fear from anything or anyone outside of their homes, but rather the men (intimate partners) in their own homes. For instance, results from the National Family Violence Resurvey of 1985, which examined overall rates of Intimate Partner Violence (IPV) among couples in the general population, indicated that about 17 percent of all U.S. couples experienced at least one episode of IPV sometime in the 12 months prior to the survey (Caetano, Schafer, & Cunradi, 2001, p. 58).

National statistics show that, "The number of violent crimes reported to law enforcement agencies in the United States decreased 1.7 percent in 2004 when compared to 2003 data. The violent crime category includes murder, forcible rape, robbery, and aggravated assault" (Uniform Crime Report, 2004, p. 1). There are statewide statistics that show that violence in the family has decreased; for example, in the State of Florida there was a decline in domestic violence from 1995 of 131,152 to 119,772 in 2004, a difference in rate of 3.3%. However, domestic violence is still prevalent in this society.

One problem with domestic violence statistics is that these numbers are only from cases being reported to law enforcement agencies. There have been extensive reports and media coverage on battered women, however few are reported. The reports in most cases are to a friend or family member. Researchers speculate that some victims of domestic violence (most commonly women) assaulted by their spouses, rarely call the police (Felson, Messner, Hoskin, & Deane, 2002). According to Felson, et al (2002) fear stems from a number of factors. These factors range from privacy issues to sympathy for the offender. These factors also include leniency on the part of the police. Black (1976) argued that the closer the victim is to the offender, the less likely he/she will report.

Background of the Study

Partner violence also has serious physical consequences for children as well as women who are battered. The psychological injuries range from severe emotional maladjustments and behavioral problems among children. These behavioral problems lead to a repetition of the violence and aggression to which they have been exposed. Evans (2005) proposed that there is extensive proof that a child witnessing domestic violence can be damaged emotionally as well as socially. According to Berry (2000) the consequences of domestic violence witnessed by children will often reach outside of the home. It affects areas of health care, criminal justice, unemployment, and social services. Berry (2000) stated, however, that perhaps the most insidious place that the damage takes place is in the minds of the young children. Children will suffer emotionally and physically as a result of witnessing any kind of domestic violence. Domestic violence has been characterized as an illness. This illness causes addictions, homelessness, suicide attempts, and even disability said Berry (2000). The consequences cause the community to give a great deal of its resources to help the victims. In addition to helping the victims of domestic violence, the community is left to also assist the perpetrators.

Aside from the physical and psychological pain associated with partner violence, there are also financial costs associated with it. Health care costs are on the rise in the domestic violence arena, and even more phenomenal among African Americans. Bent-Goodley (2004) stated that the estimated cost for partner abuse is over $44 million each year. The results are nearly 100,000 hospitalization days, emergency visits close to 30,000 each year, and almost 40,000 visits to individual physicians.

It has also been estimated that in the U.S., victim-related costs of intimate partner violence has risen to $67 billion dollars annually. Intimate partner violence victims suffer from serious health and social issues, which lead to astronomical costs (Oetzel & Duran, 2004). In addition to hospital and housing costs, there is also the cost of domestic violence telephone calls to the police, which is stated to be the largest category of telephone calls each year (Gelles & Cornell, 1990).

After 20 years of research, it has been determined that domestic violence is a very serious problem in this society. Although there has been extensive discussion and interest in domestic violence, researchers are now starting to realize that domestic violence is a complex issue among ethnic minorities (West, 1998). One category that has been overlooked is cultural differences. Explanations for the oversight include researchers using a color blind approach to domestic violence; or researchers determining that this was a problem that affected mainly the poor and ethnic minorities; to the extreme of a political gag order on battering being imposed by the minorities themselves (Crenshaw, 1994; Eng, 1995; Ho, 1990).

According to Lee, Thompson, and Mechanic (2002) current research shows that race and ethnicity are determining factors in the variety of contextual issues. Issues such as whether or not the abuser will retaliate, the amount of financial assistance available, whether or not the children have been abused, the emotional strength of the victim, and if there is support from family and friends. The differences in the way cultures view norms concerning intimate partner violence (IPV), the family unit, and when and where to find resources in the community, are as dissimilar as the people themselves. In order to determine how to react to IPV, the woman in this situation is highly influenced in her decision making process by beliefs and expectations that she and her community hold dear. Research conducted by Lee, Thompson, and Mechanic (2002) concluded that there is very little research done on IPV in rural communities or in communities of color. They also stated that there is even less research that has been completed on how to assess the needs and desires of these communities.

Statement of the Problem

Domestic violence is not new and unfortunately has been condoned by many societies through the years. McMormick (1999) stated that it is a historical fact that men have been given the right to beat their wives and have had society agreed with this practice. He also mentioned that over the years and across many cultures, spousal abuse has been legally and socially accepted. Although this problem has permeated society, McMormick (1999) stated that it has only been recently that the United States has changed laws to make arrests, prosecute and convict domestic violence perpetrators.

However, research will show that because domestic violence is a pattern behavior, it affects more than just the victim; it affects the abuser as well as a larger part of the society in which the abuse occurs.

In order to evaluate the African American business leaders' perception regarding intimate partner violence, it will be necessary to define the phenomenon of domestic violence. The legal definition for domestic violence according to Florida Statutes (1995) is any type of assault, whether physical or sexual, that results in death or physical harm to a member of the same household, whether or not they are of blood relation. Peterson and Dixon (2001) stated that domestic violence is a pattern of behavior and the goal is to control the other person. The purpose of this study is to evaluate the perceptions and attitudes of partner abuse among African American business leaders.

Significance of the Study

Domestic violence is a hard topic to study, mainly because it is such a sensitive topic. People see the effects of domestic violence, but not many people, especially those it affects directly, are willing to talk about it. The American society values its privacy. However, in recent years privacy has become a rare commodity. Bent-Goodley (2004) affirmed that domestic violence casts a negative shadow on African American families that are striving to build their communities. There are still many questions about how African Americans perceive domestic violence. This study is significant because it can help to guide interventions and programs that can help alleviate domestic violence, so that domestic violence will not have such a negative impact in the African American community.

The study on the perceptions and attitudes of domestic violence is important because our society has the responsibility of educating its citizens to help them become productive individuals. Miller and Mullens (2002) asserted that society has to become the teacher and help its citizens to destroy unwanted behavior by implementing serious sanctions for those unwanted actions. Individuals are socialized to believe and develop values held by society. While that is usually a positive aspect, there is a negative side, such as the belief system, which allows people to disregard such problems as domestic violence. Dakis (1995) insisted that society can no longer treat domestic violence as just another family matter; it must be brought to light and be dealt with openly. Miller and Mullens (2002) explained that domestic violence became monumental because of a case in the United States that initiated the change process. On July 5, 1977, a woman by the name of Carmen Bruno filed a lawsuit against then New York City Police

Departments Commissioner, Michael Cod, as well as the Probation and Family Court Department. She filed this suit because she was a victim of domestic violence and felt that she was treated unfairly when she reported that her husband had assaulted her and the police failed to arrest him. She was supported by many of the Women's groups in New York at the time. One year later, the New York Supreme Court ruled in Carmen Bruno's favor stating that "Bruno had been denied equal protection" (p. 476). Because of this lawsuit, the Police Department, as well as Probation and Family Courts, have re-written their policies and now require arrests in cases where there are visible injuries in spousal assault cases.

This study will conscientiously attempt to provide assistance to the African American Community in the Panhandle of Florida and improve the family life. When a topic of this magnitude is affecting the lives of the people in a society, it seems almost unfair not to be concerned or attempt to aid the African American society in the Panhandle of Florida in these injustices. This study will also help to extend the knowledge base of those who are interested in this topic but have limited access to African Americans perceptions about this topic, whether or not they are involved in domestic violence. This study will create new knowledge on the topic, because there will be children and teenagers, adults, as well as senior adults who may not know about this topic or have limited exposure to this topic, aside from the media.

In the social science arena, the "domino effect" occurs relating to domestic violence. It carries the proverbial domino affect due to issues inadvertently affecting other individuals. Those issues, as previously discussed being intimate partner abuse witnessed by children, children being affected outside of the home, the community relieving some of the pressure, so forth. The evaluation of this specific study of the perceptions and attitudes of African American business leaders help to narrow down some of the negative behavior in society at large. When domestic violence is reduced, the negative alcoholic behaviors will be downsized, the drug abuse will decline, and child abuse will decrease. While domestic violence intervention speculates as to how it can be reduced, if nothing is done to stop the cycle, none of the possibilities to lessen it will occur. Therefore, this topic is very relevant to the social science arena. It is especially relevant to those who work in social service agencies and are thus affected by domestic violence on a daily basis.

Purpose

The purpose of this study is to evaluate the perceptions and attitudes of partner abuse among African American business leaders. It is now widely accepted that domestic violence manifests itself and is experienced differently across race and cultural differences. However, there is still little evidence that more violence occurs in one cultural group versus another.

According to the Program for Multicultural Health: Cultural Competency (1993) from the University of Michigan, there is evidence of similarities among African Americans, Asians, and Latinos in the area of domestic violence. For example, for all three groups there are internal barriers such as the misunderstanding of how to define domestic violence, as well as the stigma that is affiliated with domestic violence. However, the differences among the cultures relating to domestic violence are apparent in our society. For example, African American women seek to maintain their family at any cost; many of these women remain with the abusive partner. Asian women want to avoid bringing shame to their family and they want to protect their family and their marriages, no matter what the cost (Program for Multicultural Health, 1993). As for the Latino group they want to preserve the unity and devotion of the family. Though, these may sound similar the differences are equally important to each group.

The following are the goals of the study:

1. Identify the perceptions and attitudes of partner abuse among African American business leaders, measured by the PADV-R.
2. Determine if characteristics such as age, socioeconomic status, occupation, and religion play a role in the perceptions and attitudes of African American business leaders.

Rationale

Partner abuse is a common occurrence among African Americans. The severity of the problem is baffling to many communities. Research into the thoughts and ideas of this aspect of the African American community will raise awareness about partner abuse. Research into the African American community about the perceptions and attitudes of domestic violence will bring forth a level of consciousness as to how culture affects domestic violence. Angel and Thoits (1987) liken the perceptions and attitudes to a template, whereas the similar characteristics are the driving force of a particular culture. This strong bond allows the members of the group to be able to depend upon one another for strength and support. Ultimately, perceptions and attitudes will help researchers to determine the factors controlling domestic violence, the reporting of domestic violence among African Americans, and how to develop culturally competent instruments.

In summary, the study will emphasize the significance of cultural competence in identifying problems of domestic violence among African American families. The attitudes and perceptions about domestic violence among African Americans also identify how African Americans attempt to solve their problems. One of the problems facing African Americans is the lack of accessibility to needed services. Bent-Goodley (2004) emphasized the issues facing African Americans; she states that many programs are out of the reach of those in need, such as shelters and the intervention programs for batterers. They are not located in the community where the people who are in need live. Additionally, when the victim has located an agency, the appointment may be missed because of the lack of reliable transportation. The African American community needs to work together in order to offer supportive and accessible services to those in need.

Research Questions

1. Among African American business leaders, are the perceptions and attitudes toward domestic violence based on the level of income in the home?
2. Among African American business leaders, are the perceptions and attitudes held toward domestic violence significantly dependent on the highest level of education completed?
3. Among African American business leaders, was there evidence that domestic violence had occurred based on their relationship with someone who has been or is still in a domestic violence relationship, as measured by the Definitions of Domestic Violence
   Scale-Revised (Yick, 1997)?
4. Among African American business leaders, is there a relationship between the perceptions of partner abuse

and various demographic variables such as: marital status, occupation, gender, religion, and age?

Definition of Terms

Intimate Partner Violence

"Is violence committed by a spouse, ex-spouse, current or former boyfriend or girlfriend? It occurs among both heterosexual and same-sex couples and is often a repeated offense" (Department of Health & Human Services, 2003, p. 9).

Panhandle

The area of Northwest Florida, which includes Panama City, Destin, Fort Walton Beach, and Pensacola.

African American Business Leaders

For the purpose of this study, the term African American Business Leaders is defined as a sample of the people listed in these two directories, Emerald Coast Black Pages, (2001-2002), published by Motez Robinson, Jr. and Harambee, the Black Business Directory of the Greater Pensacola Area, (2005), published by Unity Enterprises, Inc. The fact that these individuals were African Americans, who held prominent positions in their respective organizations, was independently verified.

Assumptions and Limitations

Everyone who agreed to participate in this study was given the definition of "intimate partner" violence. Participants of the survey also understood that no one, other than the participant, was to complete the survey. A final assumption was that everyone who received the survey was capable of comprehending what was expected within the survey. Limitations included not generalizing or coming to conclusions about other populations other than the one specified, nor to analyze the population mentioned in other geographical areas other than the ones chosen. Additional limitations include not generalizing about the reading capabilities of some of the participants. The questionnaires were sent to businesses in order to reduce the risk factor for anyone living in a household with domestic violence issues. Therefore, results may not be generalized to all African Americans because this research looked specifically at business leaders.

These assumptions and limitations are relevant to this study because the issues being discussed are issues that many people tend to avoid. Therefore, it is important for the participant to know what intimate partner violence entails in order to complete the survey in an intelligent manner. It was also important that the individual to whom the survey was mailed, was the one who completed the survey to ensure validity of the responses given. As far as limitations were concerned, the geographical area was important, since only a small region was being concentrated on at the time. It would be dishonest if other areas not intended for study were utilized and then reported falsely. The capability of the participants was important to this study because one wants to ensure that its readers will take this research seriously; therefore, the participants should be taken seriously. The researcher attempted not to make any generalizations.

Nature of the Study

The researcher will not delve into the world of child abuse, same-sex intimate partner violence, nor prevention and rehabilitation programs for batterers. There are many more areas of domestic violence and intimate partner violence. However, it would be best to maintain a small spectrum of the domestic violence scale because of the time constraints, confidentiality issues, as well as ethical issues. The nature of this study is to determine how African American business leaders perceive domestic violence as it pertains to intimate partners. The study also touches on how the African American community handles domestic violence based on the perceptions and attitudes of its members.

Organization of the Remainder of the Study

Chapter Two will discuss the appropriate literature related to the problem just described. Chapter Three will describe and discuss the research methodology selected to respond to the problem. Chapter Four will present and analyze the data collected using the methodology described in Chapter Three. The study will conclude with Chapter Five, which is a summary of conclusions drawn from the data presented in Chapter Four and will present recommendations for future research (Rossman, 1995, p. 93).

CHAPTER 2. LITERATURE REVIEW

The literature review examined domestic violence as a social problem. The comparison of the problem of domestic violence will be examined among various ethnic groups. Contrasting different theoretical frameworks will present the theories of domestic violence. The major research that has been conducted on public perceptions and attitudes of domestic violence will be highlighted. Lastly, the factors influencing domestic violence including the history and culture of the African American community will also be reviewed.

Partner Violence as a Social Problem

Scope of the Problem

In society today there is much discussion of problems relating to marital or intimate partner domestic violence. There is outrage in crimes relating to domestic violence expressed by the community at large; due to offenses that range from sexual assault, rape, and murder. However, the victims of these offenses often will tolerate an intimate partner slapping or punching them and view this as a way that the individual gets his point across. In some situations women who strike back do not consider it abuse. Ramos, Carlson, and McNutt (2001) postulated that among the women who leave their abusers and return to them, Black women are in the lead when compared to their White counterparts. Black women are also more apt to fight back and are less likely to call social services, the police, or obtain legal assistance.

Robinson (2003) asserted that the number of those who report domestic violence is only two-thirds of those who experience it. He also states that these victims have been kicked, punched, almost beaten to death, or attacked with a weapon that caused serious injury. The Centers for Disease Control and Prevention provide statistics that prove that there are at least 1.5 million women and over 800,000 men who are raped or assaulted physically by an intimate partner annually. Berlinger (2004) added that each year over 500,000 women seek medical attention for these injuries.

In a survey completed by the Commonwealth Fund in 1998, which consisted of a cross-sectional sample of women 18 years of age and older, it was determined that over four out of ten women in the U.S. are likely to have been victims of one or more of the following violent crimes: child abuse (17.8%), physical assault (19.1%), rape (20.4%), and domestic violence (34.6%). The same study indicated that violence for African American women, immigrants, and Native American women are even higher (Robinson, 2003). Sexual abuse accounts for over half of the issues women experience when they become victims of violence (Robinson, 2003). Hammett, et al, (1992) commented that among White females, homicide is only the fourth common cause of death; whereas among Black females, it is the most common cause of death, especially among ages 15-34.

Marital violence varies in forms, extending from mild verbal abuse to severe physical abuse, behavioral patterns of physical, emotional, psychological, sexual, and economic forms to perpetuate fear, intimidation, power, and control. According to the Harvard Law Review (1971) there have been stereotypes that have caused women in general to suffer. For example, the thought that women are inferior to men in the work force or women are not stable enough emotionally to handle a position of leadership or they are too weak and dainty for manual labor. The Review stated that the stereotypes even assert that women do not have a need to work, nor do they recognize the importance of a job because they are always absent or they quit shortly after they start working.

Against this background of discriminatory attitudes and costly underutilization of females, the 1964 Civil Rights Acts included sex as a prohibited criterion in employment choices. Section 703(a) declares it to be an unfair employment practice for an employer to hire, fire, or otherwise discriminate in respect to the compensation, terms, conditions, or privileges of employment because of sex; or to limit, segregate, or classify employee (Harvard Law Review, 1971, p. 1109).

Partner Violence among Minority Groups

In recent years society has come to recognize domestic violence as a problem. Many studies have been completed to determine a plethora of issues related to domestic violence. One issue about domestic violence is how it affects minority groups. When it comes to domestic violence, African American men have been researched extensively to determine the causes of violence. According to Ahn (2002) African Americans have been favored in the research studies and minority groups such as Hispanics, American Indians, and Asians have been set aside. Therefore, the following sections will give a brief description of some of the issues and problems that these groups face on a regular basis.

African Americans

Domestic violence abuse among African Americans against their intimate partner has risen dramatically over the past decade. According to Gaskin-Laniyan (2003) between 1993 and 1998; Blacks experienced intimate violence at significantly higher rates than other groups of people. Black women experience intimate violence at a rate of 35% higher than White women and 2.5% higher than other minority group women.

Some women do not believe that they are being abused because they retaliate. However, in the final analysis, many African American women will kill or be killed by their intimate partners. Unfortunately, many African Americans do not perceive domestic violence as an issue to be concerned about. Bent-Goodley (2004) concluded that

African American women are more likely to kill or be killed by an intimate partner of domestic violence than are White women. She proclaims that the reasons for this phenomenon are that some African American women don't believe they are in danger until it is too late; or they refuse to seek assistance when they realize they are in danger. The African American community must decide to make domestic violence a priority health issue so that solutions can be ascertained.

Hispanics

According to research from Lown and Vega (2001), there is not a major difference between the intimate partner violence (IPV) among Hispanics and among Whites. Lown and Vega (2001) also gave a comparative rates between Hispanics and Whites based on reports from 2000. Hispanics reported 10.5% - 17.3%, whereas Whites report 3.4% to 11.6%. Researchers have determined that for some subgroups of Hispanics, such as Mexicans, acculturation plays a big role in the perpetration of IPV. The Mexicans, having left their homes, also left their support system and extended families. This, states researchers Lown and Vega (2001), leaves them unguarded against new stressors in a new environment.

Asian Americans

In the Asian society, the man is usually considered the leader. In this patriarchal society, what the man says is law. Since what the man says is law, if a woman reported violence from her husband, she would be considered an outcast in her family. Lee, Thompson, and Mechanic (2002) stated that an Asian woman could not rely on her elderly family members to help her cope with trying to leave a violent relationship. The Asian family relies heavily on what looks good on the outside, in other words, appearance is extremely important. Ahn (2002) concluded that Asian women do not want to bring shame to their family by telling outsiders about the violence in her family.

American Indians

Robin, Chester, and Rasmussen (1998) completed a study in which they reported that 31% of the American Indian (AI) women in a Southwestern community reported some type of intimate violence the previous year. In the same study 91% of the AI women reported some type of intimate violence in their lifetime. Oetzel and Duran (2004) stated that AI women are at a higher risk for violence than other minority women and White women. They also state that American Indian women are at a higher risk than Hispanics and Whites of being murdered by their intimate partner.

Domestic Violence in the African American Community

Backgrounds of African Americans

African slavery spanned over four centuries, and over 40 million Africans were enslaved. McCollum (1997) stated that the major differences between how Africans came to America versus how other immigrants came to America were vast. A few of them are: (a) Africans came without their families, (b) they came without their own consent, (c) they came in chains, and (d) they came under subhuman travel conditions. McCullum (1997) also stated that assimilating into the new culture was frowned upon for Africans but widely accepted for other immigrants. Blackwell (1985) asserted that while Blacks were in America in the physical state they did not have the rights and privileges afforded other immigrants.

One of the reasons for having been only a minor part of this country was due to American apartheid post slavery. The role of the American apartheid seemingly gave a boost to domestic violence in an obscure way. After being freed from beatings and hangings, to be let free in a Country that was not willing to consider the Black race equal or even human could have had negative consequences that influenced the use of violence. However, there are different theories to why IPV exits, as will be discussed in the Theories of Domestic Violence section.

According to the *Merriam-Webster Online Dictionary* (2005), *apartheid* means racial segregation. It states that it is "A policy of segregation and political and economic discrimination against non-European groups in the Republic of South Africa" (2005). However, South Africa is not the only place where non-Europeans experienced Apartheid. In America, even after President Lincoln had emancipated slaves in 1863, many people, both in the North and the South felt strongly that Blacks and Whites should still be separated or worse yet, segregated.

For example, according to Cha-Jua (2001), African Americans were left out of the opportunity arena on many occasions. He stated that the 1862 Homestead Act, which offered millions of acres to Whites who were citizens of America, as well as immigrants from Europe, was not available to African Americans. In 1935, a time when the majority of Black people worked as domestic servants and farm hands, they were almost completely left out of the Social Security Act. Finally, Cha-Jua (2001) stated that for 20 years (1940 – 1960) Whites benefited from low interest housing loans offered by the Federal Housing Authority; but Blacks were excluded. These discriminatory practices have consequences for the African American family.

Traditional Family Organization and Value Orientation of African Americans

In most traditional African societies the husband is the provider. The husband made all of the decisions for the family. The perception of the role of women in society has changed in the African American culture. Many African American men have been unable to dismiss the ramifications of slavery. Feagin and Sikes (1994) made a strong proclamation that within the African tradition; the providers and the protectors of the family were the strong men, the fathers. The father was the leader of the family as well as the bloodline.

Many believe that because slavery ended a long time ago, there are no lasting effects on African American people today. Billingsley (1968) asserted that people of African descent have never been compensated in any way for the ills inflicted on African American people by slavery. The results of slavery can still be seen today as African Americans face racism, discrimination, unemployment, and many other problems. According to Brannon (1983) what started with slavery, has been perpetuated by prejudice and discrimination.

African Americans, regardless of socioeconomic level, combine historical and current experiences to define familial and external relationships. The survival of the African American people lies in their African past (Blackwell, 1985). According to Feagin and Sikes (1994), the African tradition is to hold family values high and to extend those values to the vast array of people they call family.

African Americans have traditionally found support in the extended family network and the church. Other support systems include governmental and social service agencies (Wilson & Stith, 1991). Jewell (1988) concluded that the United States stresses autonomy for individuals and families. But not many can manage without outside assistance. The Black family has had to learn to rely on society to assist them because of social barriers. Blacks rely on society in order to survive and then try to give back some type of contribution to be seen in a positive light. Regardless of socioeconomic level, African Americans take from their African heritage a tradition of strong kinship bonds, family stability, high religiosity, high regard for property ownership, and a history of political participation, activism, and social striving (Blackwell, 1985).

Wayne L. Davis, Ph.D. & Ann-Marie C. Buchanan, Ph.D.

Domestic Violence in the African American Community

Domestic violence is a serious issue in any community. However, the African American (AA) community is an especially sensitive community when it comes to violence in the home. The AA community was once seen as a very close-knit community as far as love and family were concerned. The once extended family of AAs has now, in some cases, been diminished to the nuclear family, because of reasons such as low economics, sub-standard education, crime, and subsequently, violence in the home. Malley-Morrison and Hines (2004) asserted that in many African societies, the norm was extended families, which was the basis of their foundation. This foundation provided their feelings of togetherness in political and economical issues. It was also the norm, since slavery, for Black families to take care of children of relatives or close friends on the basis of love and the family values (Malley-Morrison & Hines, 2004). Many husbands, who are unable to financially take care of their families, resort to violence as an avenue to feel better about life. The result, however, is the family and the community being torn apart. In addition, the rate of wife abuse was higher among Black families where the husband was unemployed.

Theories of Domestic Violence

Individual Theories

Berry (2000) stated that it would be wonderful if a problem could be identified and solved within a nice specific time frame. However, domestic violence does not come in a neat little package of "identify and solve." The victims are from all classes and background and domestic violence knows no boundaries.

Environmental or Situational Theories

Research conducted by Schulz, Israel, Williams, Parker, Becker, and James (2000) concluded that there have been serious factors associated with women's health issues being viewed differently than other races. These factors include discrimination, socioeconomic status, and major life events. Other researchers agreed with Schulz, et al, regarding environmental issues that jeopardize marriages. These researchers state that regarding stability in marriage, African Americans are more stressed than Whites. This is due to the lower levels of support within the marriage and also the lack of financial security (Keith & Norwood, 1997).

Psychoanalytic Instinctual Theory

Sigmund Freud was one of the theorists who viewed violence as a reaction. Muro-Ruiz (2002) contended that years ago many writers thought that man was simply aggressive naturally. Freud's first thought process was broken down into two principles of man: (a) the pleasure principle and (b) the reality principle. However, Freud eventually changed his thinking when he recognized that both principles were seeking to do the same thing, to get rid of tension. MuroRuiz (2002) stated that after World War 1 Freud changed his mind yet again and determined that man only seeks death. He stated that the instinct of death, known as Thanatos is a war between the instincts of life and death. Thanatos is viewed in two different ways; both, however, deal with destruction of life. The first way is self-destruction, which means that Thanatos is directed at self. The second confronts the barriers on the outside, which is resolved only with aggression. MuroRuiz (2002) admonished his readers not to confuse the death instinct with a desire to murder someone; he states it is just the self-destructive drive of the human being. According to this theory, IPV is an innate desire to hurt or destroy the abuser not the victim.

Social Learning Theory

There is an alternative view of Albert Bandura, known as the social learning theory. He, as well as Ross and Ross (1961) pointed that through the process of modeling, where a person learns behavior simply by watching and then imitating others, domestic violence is learned, imitated, and passed down from generation to generation. A wealth of laboratory experiences with humans lends strong validation to the claim that aggression can be learned through modeling (Bandura, Ross, & Ross, 1961). According to Muro-Ruiz (2002) Bandura viewed violence as action. There is a high price to pay for violence. The behavior of violence is constantly under attack, and there is something feeding the drive in order to maintain the negative behavior.

There is evidence that there is a relationship between domestic violence and the unemployment as well as underemployment of the male. Since the days of slavery, the African American woman has had to take on the role of the breadwinner. This undertaking has given the man in the home a bruised ego because not only is his wife working, but also she may be making more money than him, if he has a job. According to Slack and Jensen (2002), in 1991 Gene F. Summers, the President of the Rural Sociological Society, challenged rural sociologists to determine the reasons why minorities who live in rural communities have problems getting affordable and decent housing, good health care, good education, and decent paying jobs. Many African American men are either unemployed or underemployed and some use this situation as justification to abuse their intimate female partner. Rankin completed a study in 1991 that indicated that, compared to many places, Blacks living in the Black Belt, located in the some Southern States, such as Alabama, Florida, and Mississippi, made less money than Whites. The issues of unemployment as well as underemployment are used to justify much of the abuse African American women endure. Gamache (1998) asserted that because of the perception that minority men hold, that they have little or no power in society. Thus, they demand respect from their partners. He continues that for these reasons women of color experience higher rates of battering than other women.

Women suffer from various types of violence at the hands of intimate partners, but it appears that society has become insensitive to it all for reasons unbeknownst to many in society itself. Berry (2000) believed that society has become too desensitized to all types of brutality. There is violence all around; on TV it is prevalent in the news, sports, and the many programs watched daily. Also televised are the wars that this country engages in, violence all around. Because of the violence viewed on the outside, it is easier to accept violence in the home.

Structural/Cultural Theories

Key words such as equality and empowerment are words many battered women do not hear on a regular basis. But it is this society's responsibility to educate women of all races that they can achieve gender equality and be empowered to have a better life. It is vital that women receive secondary education stated Grown, Gupta, and Pande (2005) in order to assist in reducing the violence against women. Violence against women perpetuates serious health issues such as sexually transmitted diseases, unwanted pregnancies, and pregnancies that have major complications. Caracci (2003) voiced his opinion at the Convention on the Elimination of Discrimination against Women by stating that first the tolerance of violence against women must be understood through cultural factors. Then the United States must act appropriately in order to train men and women in the proper way to behave in a relationship. This should be done in hopes of eliminating stereotypes that perpetuate discrimination and feelings of being lower or higher than anyone else.

Wayne L. Davis, Ph.D. & Ann-Marie C. Buchanan, Ph.D.

Perceptions of and Attitudes toward Domestic Violence

Definitions of Domestic Violence

One definition that Berry (2000) used to describe domestic violence is any abusive treatment. She stated that if a woman chooses to lower her standards by accepting an attack on her self-esteem, then she has put herself as a target for more assaults. She told of a story told by Dr. Forward. Berry (2000) stated that the woman was shocked that her partner thought he could hit her and get away with it. So she told him that she would leave him if he did it again. He did it a few days later and she left him. Again Berry (2000) emphasized that women should stand up for themselves.

Contextual Justification for Domestic Violence

Justification for domestic violence on the part of the woman usually becomes an issue when children are involved. When women realize that their children are at risk, they are more apt to fight back or to defend themselves.

One form of explanation for the man is retribution, mainly because of adultery. When the male ego is attacked, he feels justified abusing his wife, especially if she cheated on him. Some men find themselves justified in other areas such as the woman flirting, being intoxicated, or nagging. Greenblat (1985) stated that 16% of respondents accepted the use of some type of aggression when there is proof of a wife's infidelity.

Factors Contributing to Domestic Violence

Socioeconomic Factors

Studies indicate that socioeconomic factors affect the level of spousal abuse in the African American community. Some researchers believe that socioeconomic status (SES) is not a major factor in abuse between races.

Ramos, Carlson, and McNutt (2004) state that in a mental health report issues by the U.S. Surgeon General in 1999, there were major differences between the health issues of Blacks and Whites. Ramos, et al (2004) state that there are also researchers who report that there are no differences in the level of distress between the two groups. They also state that there is little research on the reasons for anxiety and depression among Black women.

Straus and his colleagues maintained that, based on sociological theories of family violence, that social and structural factors impact domestic violence (Straus, 1980). Straus, Gelles, and Steinmetz (1980) state that the age, level of education, and the income of an individual is variables that are linked to domestic violence. Because of the economic instability that accompanies low income, Straus, et al (1980) state that individuals from low-income groups are more susceptible to domestic violence.

Attitudes toward Acceptance of Marital Violence

Many couples accept that in marriage there will be a certain amount of aggression. In summary, some researchers view attitudes of tolerance of domestic violence as the leading cause of domestic violence. Others believe that there is a correlation between attitudes toward domestic violence and actual incidences of violent behavior.

CHAPTER 3. METHODOLOGY

The purpose of this study was to evaluate the perceptions and attitudes of partner abuse among African American business leaders. This chapter gives information regarding the procedures that were utilized to conduct this study. The methodology of the study is organized in the following sections: (1) research design, (2) population and sample, (3) instrumentation, (4) data collection procedures, and (5) data analysis.

Research Design

This study consisted of a correlational survey design utilizing a cross-sectional survey technique. Due to the sensitivity and possible danger associated with domestic violence, an experimental component was not feasible.

Rationale

The quantitative approach was selected in order to explain and predict the perception and attitudes of partner abuse among African American business leaders. This study analyzed the known variables by utilizing deductive analysis in an attempt to prove the hypotheses.

Population and Sample

The target population for this study was defined as African American business leaders. The accessible population was defined as African American business leaders, eighteen years of age and older, who were currently residing in the Panhandle of Florida, which consists of: Panama City, Destin, Fort Walton Beach, and Pensacola. They were surveyed via mail to determine their perceptions and attitudes of domestic violence amongst intimate partners. This study replicated one completed by Dr. Bonnie Ahn in 2002. Dr. Ahn studied Asian Americans in Baton Rouge, Louisiana. Domestic violence is such an important issue in society that it demands constant research. However, it is sometimes difficult to locate people who are willing to participate in such research. The research completed by Bonnie Ahn showed that there is a way to retrieve the necessary information while still protecting the participants' privacy and preserving their confidentiality, in order to determine how this serious topic affects African American business leaders.

The frame of accessible population was established by utilizing two African American directories: Emerald Coast Black Pages, (2001–2002), published by Motez Robinson, Jr. and Harambee, the Black Business Directory of the Greater Pensacola Area, (2005), published by Unity Enterprises, Inc. A sample of 152 African American business leaders were asked to participate in the study, via survey. The surveys were mailed to the businesses and the person or position named in the directories was requested to complete the survey. Utilizing a RaoSoft Sample Size Calculator system, it was determined that with a sample size of 152, the minimum acceptable number was approximately 47. An acceptable margin of error was 10%. Participants were included because they met the following criteria: (1) they had to be adult, age 18 and older, (2) they had to live in the Panhandle of Florida at the time of completing the survey, and (3) they had to identify themselves as African American.

Instrumentation

A two-part instrument was utilized for data collection (Research Instrument, Appendix A). Part I of the instrument consisted of a measure of the perceptions and attitudes toward domestic violence: The Perceptions of and Attitudes Toward Domestic Violence Questionnaire-Revised (PADV-R), developed by Yick (1997). Part II of the instrument is the Participation Profile form (Ahn, 2002). This survey should have taken approximately 20 minutes to complete.

Validity and Reliability

These instruments have proven to be valid and reliable by being utilized at least two times in the past. The internal consistency reliability form was applicable in the previous two researches because one instrument yielded very similar results (Leedy & Ormrod, 2016). The originator of the instrument, Dr. Alice Yick Flanagan, conducted the first test. The second was conducted by Dr. Bonnie Ahn, which this current study is replicating. Face validity would be the form that this instrument utilizes as it measures specific characteristics of the participants in this study (Leedy & Ormrod, 2016). Both stated that they found the instruments to be accurate and trustworthy in identifying the perceptions and attitudes toward domestic violence. Since these instruments were utilized at least two times in the past, it would seem that this researcher would be able to retrieve similar responses even with a different population.

In order to have validated this study for use with African American business leaders, the instrument was revised. In the original questionnaire, Section III, questions "d" and "e" referred to Koreans, therefore, they have been omitted. In Section V, the first question was adjusted to say African American friends and family. And in Section VI, question four was omitted and in question eight Buddhism and Confucianism were removed as choices.

The Perceptions of and Attitudes toward Domestic Violence Questionnaire – Revised (PADV-R). The PADV-R is the instrument designed to measure perceptions of and attitudes toward domestic violence. Permission was received to use this instrument (Appendix D). The purpose of the PADV-R is to measure a variety of domestic violence concepts, such as definitions of domestic violence, participants' attitude about domestic violence, the reasons for domestic violence, any myths about domestic violence, as well as why people justify domestic violence (Ahn 2002). The PADV-R is an effective instrument to utilize for measuring how the African American population perceives domestic violence.

Definitions of Domestic Violence

The measurement tool that was utilized is the Definitions of Domestic Violence ScaleRevised (Yick, 1997). This scale measures the participants' concept of domestic violence with regard to certain physical, psychological, and/or sexual acts of aggression considered violent against spouses. Yick (1997) reported that the Cronbach's alpha for this scale in her study was 0.82. The Cronbach's alpha Internal Consistency Coefficient of this scale for this study was determined to be 0.93. This scale consists of three subscales.

According to Ahn (2002) the three subscales that comprise this scale are used to measure physical aggression, psychological aggression, and sexual abuse. The subscales measured the attitudes of the participants as they determined what they consider domestic violence among the choices listed. The measurements ranged from strongly agree to strongly disagree and numbers will be chosen from 1-6 respectively. There are items in this section used mainly as a tool to separate the domestic violence questions from the ones not necessarily pertaining to domestic violence.

Attitudes Toward the Use of Interpersonal Violence

The Attitudes Toward the Use of Interpersonal Violence-Revised Scale measured respondents' attitudes toward the use of violence in various situations. The subscales utilized in this section were put in place to measure the use of physical force on the part of the abuser in order to solve issues and problems in the home. All questions used the Likert-type scale, which ranges from 1-6, *strongly agree to strongly disagree.*

Causes of Domestic Violence

The Causes of Domestic Violence-Revised Scale measured individuals' beliefs regarding the factors that precipitate domestic violence. Three sub-scales comprise the Causes of Domestic Violence Revised Scale. These three sub-scales were put in place to determine whether or not there are cultural, environmental, or individual factors that cause domestic violence. They were measured using the Likert-type scale.

Participation Profile Form

The second part of the instrument completed by the participant was the Participation Profile Form. It collected demographic information (Ahn, 2002). The characteristics of this form included: gender, age, marital status, occupation, household income, educational status, and religion.

Data Collection Procedure

The PADV-R two-part instrument was utilized for data collection. The data collection process took place over a three-month period between May 2006 and July 2006. A list of approximately 152 African American business leaders from the Emerald Coast Black Pages, which consisted of businesses mainly in Panama City and Pensacola (2001-2002), the Harambee (2005) the Black Business Directory of the Greater Pensacola Area were utilized. An introductory letter, a copy of the Information about Research Participants' Rights, a copy of the instrument (Appendix B), and a list of Domestic Violence Contact Information were mailed to all 152 African American business leaders with a stamped, self-addressed return envelope. The researcher's name, P.O. Box address, and work telephone number were listed in the letter in case there were any questions.

Approximately 10 days after the first mailing, a reminder post card was mailed to all participants. After 10 more days, telephone calls were made to the business phone listed in the directory to those participants who did not return the completed instrument. Researcher mailed another set of study instruments to anyone who wanted to participate but lost the original one.

Research Questions

1. Among African American business leaders, are the perceptions and attitudes toward domestic violence based on the level of income in the home?
2. Among African American business leaders, are the perceptions and attitudes held toward domestic violence significantly dependent on the highest level of education completed?
3. Among African American business leaders, was there evidence that domestic violence had occurred based on their relationship with someone who has been or is still in a domestic violence relationship, as measured by the Definitions of Domestic Violence
   Scale-Revised (Yick, 1997)?
4. Among African American business leaders, is there a relationship between the perceptions of partner abuse and various demographic variables such as: marital status, occupation, gender, religion, and age?

Data Analysis

The SPSS Data Analysis System was utilized to analyze the data. The mean PADV-R score was calculated for each participant. Analysis of Variance (ANOVA) tests were conducted on the data comparing the mean PADV-R response of participants with demographic factors, including age, gender, marital status, religion, education level, occupation, and household income. If ANOVA results indicated that a significant difference existed for mean

PADV-R scores for variables with more than two groups, post-hoc pairwise comparisons using the Least Significant Difference (LSD) method were conducted to determine which groups had different mean PADV-R scores. A reliability analysis was used to analyze the participants' responses for Sections I through IV of the survey for internal consistency. The results of the reliability analysis indicate that the data is highly consistent for all 51 of the questions in Sections I through IV (Cronbach's alpha = 0.93). Nunnaly (1978) considers 0.7 to be an acceptable reliability coefficient.

Ethical Considerations

A major part of ethics in research is confidentiality, which "can be defined as explicit or implied guarantee by a researcher to a respondent in social science research whereby the respondent is confident that any information provided to the researcher cannot be attributed back to that respondent" (Jamison, 1999, p.1). Explicit confidentiality is where the researcher supplies the participant with both written and verbal notices to explain what will be done throughout the planned study. With explicit confidentiality, the researcher clearly informs the participant of the many levels of disclosure that can be negotiated between the researcher and the participant. Jamison (1999) stated that the levels can range anywhere from utter and complete disclosure to promising complete anonymity to the participant.

If ethics is not in the forefront of the researcher's mind, then problems may occur. "Epidemiological research involving people's lives, involves inherent risks. There are issues of confidentiality, problems of disclosure, and the need to ensure adequate and informed consent" (Ellsberg & Heise, 2002, p. 1599). There is a definite role that ethics has in research and all researchers hold fast to an ethical way of life. Many times innocent participants will be the unsuspecting victims who suffer because of the researcher's unethical behavior.

Domestic violence is a serious topic. It is also a very sensitive topic and the realization that participants will be reluctant to cooperate is great. Therefore, it is this researcher's intent to abide by several ethical standards, which include informing the participants that all the information they disclose on the survey will be kept strictly confidential. Researcher will also inform the participants that the information collected will not contain names or the location of the participants. The numbers on the survey will only be utilized to show how many people participated in the study and the answers to the questions will be in a variety of codes. The participants were treated with the utmost confidentiality. After careful review, utilizing the zoning codes of the cities, business versus residential, of the location of the businesses in the Panhandle of Florida, it was determined that 79% of the addresses in the two directories being utilized were home-based businesses. According to the review, the majority of the participants receiving the surveys were businesses. Therefore, there were no ethical issues raised regarding keeping the women who are possible victims of domestic violence safe. There were no elements in the surveys that caused undue harm to participants.

According to Parker and Ulrich (1990), when researching domestic violence among women, the women's safety should be the researcher's primary concern. The concern for safety is needed because the abuser may choose to retaliate if he has determined that his secret is no longer 'safe' with his partner, the victim. An attempt to contact a domestic violence victim may put her in danger because of the retaliation possibilities of the abuser. Therefore, it is imperative that the researcher utilizes caution when soliciting the public for participants. For this research project, the surveys were sent to businesses in the areas specified. This minimized spouses or partners finding a survey lying around the house, whereby possibly putting the female in danger. Parker and Ulrich (1990) stated that the victim may inadvertently give information that she would not normally give and put herself at risk. Many of the questions that were deemed dangerous to a woman completing this survey, were omitted, in an attempt to safeguard the participant.

According to Ellsberg and Heise (2002) a researcher must respect the participants, attempt to minimize harm, maximize the benefits, and seek justice for the participants. The researchers admit that even though no one has completed a study to figure out how often negative results are encountered with the domestic violence population, many have recognized that the women that agreed to help them with the study were at risk due to lack of attention on the part of the researcher. Ellsberg and Heise (2002) warned researchers to try not to complete face-to-face interviews with men and women in the same community if it can be avoided. The surveys were mailed to businesses and face-to-face interviews were conducted. The benefit of this study is that the information collected will assist service providers and policy makers in understanding perceptions toward domestic violence in the African American community so that they can help this community more effectively. The results of this study will benefit society, as the findings will be used to make recommendations about policies and interventions. Ellsberg and Heise (2002) encouraged researchers to try to give the participants benefits that they can actually utilize, such valuable information as to how to get out of the current violent situation or paying them for their services. For this study payment will not be an option. However, if the participant requests information for herself or himself or for a friend, it will be provided.

The study risks may range from the survey asking some sensitive questions, which may make participants feel uncomfortable to the other end of the spectrum, putting the participant in danger if the abuser found the instrument. To minimize risk, the surveys were being sent to a business address. It is also recommended that the participant does not discuss answers with spouse or significant other. Because of the nature of this topic, the risk of participants experiencing negative thoughts and feelings when completing this questionnaire is valid. Participants are informed not to put names anywhere in the survey to ensure anonymity. Identification numbers used on the instruments will be assigned to each of the participants' original individual identification numbers to add a layer of anonymity to the participants. The original mailing list with names will only be referenced for non-response follow-up mailings. Every effort will be made to maintain the confidentiality of the study records. Files will be kept in secure cabinets to which only the researchers have access.

A signed consent form in domestic violence studies could heighten a potential victim's level of danger because if a perpetrator discovers the consent form, he might retaliate (Yick, In Press). Langford (2001) noted that many institutional review boards have taken into account the unique circumstances in domestic violence cases and do not require signatures; instead, the researcher may merely be asked to provide an information sheet about the nature of the study and information about research participants' rights.

CHAPTER 4. FINDINGS

This chapter presents the participant characteristics, profile, and demographic variables. The chapter also presents the findings of each statistical test. The results are organized by the research questions.

Participant Characteristics

The instrument was mailed to the sample of 152 African American business leaders at their place of business. During the data collection, one survey was returned because the company had moved with no forwarding address, reducing the sample to 151. A total of 43 African American business leaders (28%) responded to the survey. The participants were measured by the following characteristics: age, occupation, religion, level of education, level of income, and marital status.

Participant Profile/Demographic Variables

Research Questions

1. Among African American business leaders, are the perceptions and attitudes toward domestic violence based on the level of income in the home?
2. Among African American business leaders, are the perceptions and attitudes held toward domestic violence significantly dependent on the highest level of education completed?
3. Among African American business leaders, was there evidence that domestic violence had occurred based on their relationship with someone who has been or is still in a domestic violence relationship, as measured by the Definitions of Domestic Violence Scale-Revised (Yick, 1997)?
4. Among African American business leaders, is there a relationship between the perceptions of partner abuse

and various demographic variables such as: marital status, occupation, gender, religion, and age?

In order to address these four research questions, the following hypotheses were tested.

Research Question One

The goal of the first research question was to determine if the perceptions and attitudes toward domestic violence among African American business leaders was based on the level of income in the home. The null hypothesis associated with this research question is that there is no difference between the mean PADV-R score for participants depending upon their income level. The income data was obtained through one of the questions on the survey that asked the participants to state the approximate annual household income.

Participant Income Levels

The mean PADV-R score for participants earning less than $25,000 was 2.63 with a standard deviation of 0.98, meaning that the participants *agreed*. The mean PADV-R score for participants earning between $25,000 and $50,000 was 3.60 with a standard deviation of 0.39 and the mean PADV-R score for participants that earn between $50,000 and $75,000 was 3.43 with a standard deviation of 0.41 (Table 1), which means that these participants *agreed somewhat*. In addition, the mean PADV-R score for participants that earn between $75,000 and $100,00 was 4.39 with a standard deviation of 0.85 and participants that earn $100,000 or more had a mean PADV-R score of 3.78 with a standard deviation of 0.66 (Table 1), which means that these participants *disagreed somewhat*. The results of the Analysis of Variance (ANOVA) for various income levels indicate that there is enough evidence to reject the null hypothesis (p-value = 0.006, Table 2). Therefore, there is a significant difference in the mean PADV-R score for participants of various income levels.

Table 1

Descriptive statistics for PADV-R for participants of various income levels

	n	Mean	SD	95% Confidence Interval for Mean		Minimum	Maximum
				Lower Bound	Upper Bound		
< $25,000	3	2.6270	.98157	.1886	5.0653	1.85	3.73
$25,000-49,999	11	3.6002	.38695	3.3402	3.8601	3.02	4.42
$50,000-74,999	9	3.4385	.41267	3.1213	3.7557	2.90	4.26
$75,000-99,999	4	4.3934	.84721	3.0453	5.7415	3.30	5.35
≥ $100,000	7	3.7771	.65638	3.1701	4.3842	3.08	5.10
Total	34	3.6013	.68174	3.3634	3.8391	1.85	5.35

Table 2

ANOVA for PADV-R mean for participants of various income levels

	Sum of Squares	df	Mean Square	F	Sig.
Between Groups	5.813	4	1.453	4.424	.006*
Within Groups	9.525	29	.328		
Total	15.338	33			

*The mean difference is significant at the .05 level

The results of the post-hoc pairwise comparisons for the mean PADV-R scores for the various income levels indicates that the participants earning less than $25,000 had significantly different mean PADV-R scores than participants from all the other income level categories: $25,000 - 49,999, $50,000 – 74,999, $75,000 - 99,999, and $100,000 or over (Table 3). In addition, the results of the post-hoc pairwise comparisons for the mean PADV-R scores for the various income levels indicates that the participants earning $25,000 - $49,999 had significantly different mean PADV-R scores than participants earning $75,000 - $99,999 (Table 3). Lastly, the results of the post-hoc pairwise comparisons for the mean PADV-R scores for the various income levels indicates that the participants earning $50,000 - $74,999 had significantly different mean PADV-R scores than participants earning $75,000 - $99,999 (Table 3). Therefore, the PADV-R scores differed for participants of various income levels, such that the participants in the lowest income category of less than $25,000 *agreed* with the statements about what constitutes domestic violence, whereas the middle income brackets of $25,000 – $49,999 and $50,000 – $74,999 only *agreed somewhat* with the statements about what constitutes domestic violence and the highest income brackets of $75,000 – $99,999 and over $100,000 *somewhat disagreed* with the statements about what constitutes domestic violence.

In addition to the mean PADV-R score being significantly different for participants of various income levels, the results of the Analysis of Variance (ANOVA) for Section IV of the PADV-R indicate that there is enough evidence to reject the null hypothesis (p-value = 0.038, Table 4). Therefore, there was a significant difference in the mean score for Section IV of the PADV-R for participants of various income levels. The mean score for section IV of the PADV-R ranged from 3.18 for participants earning less than $25,000 to 5.70 for participants earning $75,000 - $99,999.

Table 3

Pairwise comparisons using the Least Significant Difference (LSD) method

Income Range 4 (I)	Income Range 4 (J)	Mean Difference (I) – (J)	SE	Sig.	95% Confidence Interval Lower Bound	Upper Bound
< $25,000	$25,000-49,999	-.9732	.37328	.014*	-1.7367	-.2098
	$50,000-74,999	-.8116	.38207	.042*	-1.5930	-.0302
	$75,000-99,999	-1.7664	.43771	.000*	-2.6617	-.8712
	≥ $100,000	-1.1502	.39548	.007*	-1.9590	-.3413
$25,000-49,999	< $25,000	-.9732	.37328	.014*	.2098	1.7367
	$50,000-74,999	.1617	.25759	.535	-.3652	.6885
	$75,000-99,999	-.7932	.33462	.025*	-1.4776	-.1088
	≥ $100,000	-.1769	.27709	.528	-.7437	.3898
$50,000-74,999	< $25,000	.8116	.38207	.042*	.0302	1.5930
	$25,000-49,999	-.1617	.25759	.535	-.6885	.3652
	$75,000-99,999	-.9549	.34439	.010*	-1.6592	-.2505
	≥ $100,000	-.3386	.28882	.251	-.9293	.2521
$75,000-99,999	< $25,000	1.7664	.43771	.000*	.8712	2.6617
	$25,000-49,999	.7932	.33462	.025*	.1088	1.4776
	$50,000-74,999	.9549	.34439	.010*	.2505	1.6592
	≥ $100,000	.6163	.35921	.097*	-.1184	1.3509
≥ $100,000	< $25,000	1.1502	.39548	.007*	.3413	1.9590
	$25,000-49,999	.1769	.27709	.528	-.3898	.7437
	$50,000-74,999	.3386	.28882	.251	-.2521	.9293
	$75,000-99,999	-.6163	.35921	.097*	-1.3509	.1184

*The mean difference is significant at the .05 level

Table 4

ANOVA for Section IV mean for participants of various income levels

	Sum of Squares	df	Mean Square	F	Sig.
Between Groups	12.703	4	3.176	2.920	.038*
Within Groups	31.537	29	1.087		
Total	44.240	33			

*The mean difference is significant at the .05 level

Therefore, this research study shows that income levels make a difference in the perceptions and attitudes of domestic violence. Those participants earning below $25,000 *agreed* that behaviors such as hitting, trying to control one's life, not allowing partner to make any decisions, pushing one's partner, and others are viewed as domestic violence. While those in the other income categories *agreed somewhat* that the above behaviors constitute domestic violence, the participants in the $75,000 – $99,999 bracket *disagreed somewhat* that those behaviors described in the survey constituted domestic violence.

One can conclude that by the results of the income levels that there are differences in the perceptions and attitudes of partner abuse among African American business leaders regarding partner abuse. These differences seem to stem from the differences in the amount of money made annually. Seemingly, the less money one makes, the more aware one is of what constitutes partner abuse. The more money one makes, the more tolerable one may be of certain behaviors that are considered to be partner abuse. This may be a result of the desire to maintain a certain lifestyle, or because he or she is just not aware of what behaviors are considered partner abuse. If the latter is true, then education within the community is of the utmost importance.

Research Question Two

The purpose of the second research question was to determine if the perceptions and attitudes held toward domestic violence among African American business leaders would depend significantly on the highest level of education completed. The assumption was that the higher the level of education, the less tolerant the respondent would be of domestic violence. The belief held is that education was one of the characteristics that would help determine the perception and attitudes toward domestic violence. The null hypothesis associated with this research question was that there was no difference between the mean PADV-R score for participants depending upon their education level. The participants were asked to choose, from the list of seven categories given on the questionnaire, the highest level of education they had achieved.

The mean PADV-R score for participants with high school degrees was 3.57 with a standard deviation of 1.06, while the mean PADV-R score for participants with junior college degrees was 3.67 with a standard deviation of 0.70 and the mean PADV-R score for participants with Bachelor's degrees was 3.87 with a standard deviation of 0.70 (Table 5). In addition, the mean PADV-R score for participants with Master's degrees was 3.49 with a standard deviation of 0.41 and participants with Doctoral degrees had a mean PADV-R score of 3.71 with a standard deviation of 0.12 (Table 5). The scores for all of these participants ranged between *somewhat agree* and *somewhat disagree*. The results of the Analysis of Variance (ANOVA) for various education levels indicated that there was not enough evidence to reject the null hypothesis (p-value = 0.84, Table 6). Therefore, there was not a significant difference in the mean PADV-R score for participants of various education levels. So, from this study, it was concluded that the level of education did not influence the perceptions of and attitudes toward domestic violence for African American business leaders.

It was hypothesized that education would make a difference in the perceptions and attitudes of African American business leaders toward partner abuse. However, according to the results, even if a person did not complete high school or at the other end of the spectrum, has received a doctoral degree, it is not necessarily a determining factor of his or her thoughts about partner abuse. These results are important because they indicate that formal education is not one of the factors that contribute to domestic violence. However, further educating the African American community about the behaviors that are considered domestic violence is an essential role for the community leaders.

Table 5

Descriptive statistics for PADV-R for participants of various education levels

	n	Mean	*SD*	95% Confidence Interval for Mean		Minimum	Maximum
				Lower Bound	Upper Bound		
< High School	1	2.9786	.	.	.	2.98	2.98
High School Diploma (or equivalent)	9	3.5675	1.06214	2.7510	4.3839	1.85	5.63
Junior College Degree (A.A.)	11	3.6724	.69968	3.2023	4.1424	2.90	5.10
Bachelor's Degree (B.A., B.S.)	9	3.8713	.70057	3.3328	4.4098	3.23	5.35
Master's Degree (M.A., M.S.)	8	3.4915	.41026	3.1485	3.8345	3.08	4.32
Doctorate (Ph.D.)	3	3.7092	.11597	3.4211	3.9973	3.63	3.84
Professional (M.D., J.D., etc.)	2	4.0090	.03101	3.7304	4.2877	3.99	4.03
Total	43	3.6605	.69823	3.4456	3.8754	1.85	5.63

Table 6

ANOVA for PADV-R mean for participants of various education levels

	Sum of Squares	df	Mean Square	F	Sig.
Between Groups	1.423	6	.237	.448	.842
Within Groups	19.053	36	.529		
Total	20.476	42			

Research Question Three

The third research question inquired among African American business leaders as to whether there was there evidence that domestic violence had occurred based on their relationship with someone who has been or is still in a domestic violence relationship, as measured by the Definitions of Domestic Violence Scale-Revised (Yick, 1997). Of the 43 participants, 39 of them responded *yes* to at least one question in Section V of the PADV-R survey, which indicated that they had been told or known of any African American friends or family members who have experienced physical or verbal abuse. Of the 39 participants that responded *yes* to at least one of the Section V questions, 13 of them responded *yes* to all six questions in the section, 8 of them responded *yes* to five of the six questions, 4 of them responded *yes* to four of the six questions, 4 of them responded *yes* to three of the six questions, 4 of them responded *yes* to two of the six questions, and 6 of them responded *yes* to one of the six questions (Fig. 1). These results indicate that almost everyone who completed a questionnaire was told or knew of an African American friend or family member who had experienced physical or verbal abuse. This number is too high and indicates that there is still a lot of work to be done to stop partner abuse.

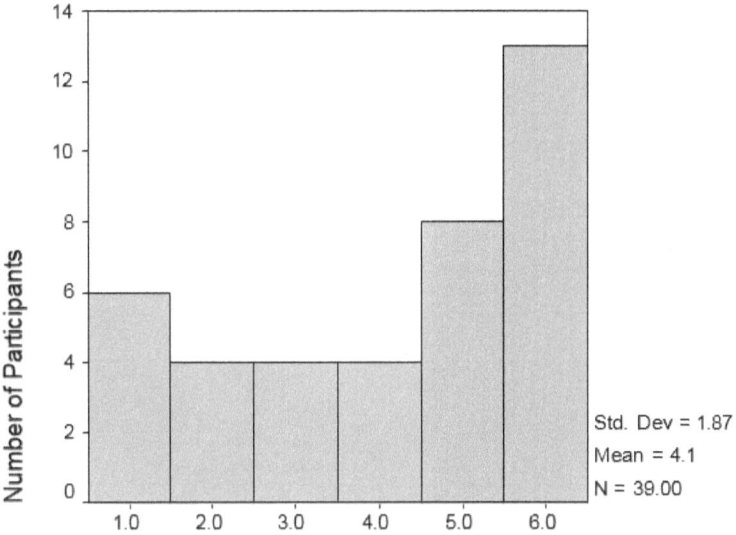

Number of Yes Responses for Section V Questions

Figure 1. Frequency Distribution for the Number of *Yes* Response to Section V Questions.

Research Question Four

Research question number four determined that among African American business leaders there was a relationship between the perceptions of partner abuse and various demographic variables such as marital status, occupation, gender, religion, and age.

Gender of Participants

The participants were asked to indicate their gender. Of the 43 participants 20 (46.5%) were men and 23 (53.5%) were women. The mean PADV-R score for male participants was 3.63 with a standard deviation of 0.56, while the mean PADV-R score for female participants was 3.69 with a standard deviation of 0.81 (Table 7). The results of the Analysis of Variance (ANOVA) for males and females indicate that there is not enough evidence to reject the null hypothesis (p–value = 0.77, Table 8). Therefore, there is not a significant difference in the mean PADV-R score for males and females.

Table 7

Descriptive statistics for PADV-R for males and females

	n	Mean	SD	95% Confidence Interval for Mean		Minimum	Maximum
				Lower Bound	Upper Bound		
Male	20	3.6261	.55713	3.3654	3.8869	2.90	5.35
Female	23	3.6904	.81280	3.3389	4.0418	1.85	5.63
Total	43	3.6605	.69823	3.4456	3.8754	1.85	5.63

Table 8

ANOVA for PADV-R mean by males and females

	Sum of Squares	*df*	Mean Square	*F*	Sig.
Between Groups	.044	1	.044	.089	.768
Within Groups	20.432	41	.498		
Total	20.476	42			

According to the results of the ANOVA, there was not a significant difference in the attitudes and perceptions among African American business leaders regarding partner abuse between males and females. This means that that the attitudes toward and perceptions of domestic violence for African American men and women are not significantly different, which indicates that gender is not an influencing factor.

Age of Participants

Participants were asked to give their age as a part of the questionnaire. The mean PADVR score for participants less than 50 years of age was 3.72 with a standard deviation of 0.86, while the mean PADV-R score for participants 50 and over was 3.62 with a standard deviation of 0.59 (Table 9). The results of the Analysis of Variance (ANOVA) for the age groups indicate that there is not enough evidence to reject the null hypothesis (p-value = 0.68, Table 10). Therefore, there is not a significant difference in the mean PADV-R score for the two age groups.

Table 9

Descriptive statistics for PADV-R by age groups

	n	Mean	SD	95% Confidence Interval for Mean		Minimum	Maximum
< 50	17	3.7158	.85832	3.2745	4.1571	1.85	5.63
≥ 50	26	3.6243	.58659	3.3874	3.8612	2.30	5.10
Total	43	3.6605	.69823	3.4456	3.8754	1.85	5.63

Table 10

ANOVA for PADV-R mean by age group

	Sum of Squares	df	Mean Square	F	Sig.
Between Groups	.086	1	.086	.173	.679
Within Groups	20.390	41	.497		
Total	20.476	42			

The participants who were under 50 years of age and the ones who were over 50 years of age had almost the same ideas and thoughts about partner abuse, and the mean PADV-R scores for these groups indicate that they *somewhat disagreed* with the statements about what constitutes domestic violence. However, even though there were no significant differences in the mean PADV-R scores, the results prove that people of all ages are in need of education about the behaviors that constitute partner abuse.

Marital Status of Participants

The mean PADV-R score for married participants was 3.62 with a standard deviation of 0.64, while the mean PADV-R score for unmarried participants was 3.74 with a standard deviation of 0.82 (Table 11). The results of the Analysis of Variance (ANOVA) for marital status indicate that there is not enough evidence to reject the null hypothesis (p-value = 0.58, Table 12). Therefore, there is not a significant difference in the mean PADV-R score for married and unmarried participants, and the mean PADV-R scores for these groups indicate that they *somewhat disagreed* with the statements about what constitutes domestic violence.

Table 11

Descriptive statistics for PADV-R for married and unmarried participants

	n	Mean	SD	95% Confidence Interval for Mean		Minimum	Maximum
				Lower Bound	Upper Bound		
Married	29	3.6184	.64070	3.3747	3.8622	2.30	5.35
Unmarried	14	3.7476	.82390	3.2719	4.2233	1.85	5.63
Total	43	3.6605	.69823	3.4456	3.8754	1.85	5.63

Table 12

ANOVA for PADV-R mean for married and unmarried participants.

	Sum of Squares	*df*	Mean Square	*F*	Sig.
Between Groups	.157	1	.157	.318	.576
Within Groups	20.318	41	.496		
Total	20.476	42			

Unmarried individuals without proper domestic violence education become married couples without proper domestic violence education. This may be the reason why there were no significant differences between the unmarried and the married participants. It shows, again, that educating the community is vital and urgent.

Occupation of Participants

The questionnaire required that the participants to circle one of the nine choices to indicate their specific occupation. The mean PADV-R score for unemployed participants was 3.56 with a standard deviation of 0.31, while the mean PADV-R score for self-employed participants was 3.72 with a standard deviation of 0.52 and the mean PADV-R score for participants that are clerical workers or salespeople was 3.98 with a standard deviation of 0.94 (Table 13). In addition, the mean PADV-R score for participants that are semi-professionals or managers was 3.48 with a standard deviation of 0.52 and participants that are professionals had a mean PADV-R score of 3.85 with a standard deviation of 0.67 (Table 13). The results of the Analysis of Variance (ANOVA) for various occupations indicate that there is not enough evidence to reject the null hypothesis (p-value = 0.09, Table 14). Therefore, there is not a significant difference in the mean PADV-R score for participants of various occupations.

Table 13

Descriptive statistics for PADV-R for participants of various occupations

	n	Mean	SD	95% Confidence Interval for Mean		Minimum	Maximum
				Lower Bound	Upper Bound		
Unemployed	7	3.5594	.30645	3.2760	3.8428	2.98	3.95
Housewife	1	2.2976	.	.	.	2.30	2.30
Skilled Labor	2	2.7105	1.21356	-8.1929	13.6139	1.85	3.57
Clerical, Salesperson	5	3.9834	.93683	2.8201	5.1466	3.38	5.63
Semi-Professional, Manager	7	3.4808	.51622	3.0034	3.9582	2.90	4.42
Professional	18	3.8510	.67041	3.5177	4.1844	3.02	5.35
Self-employed	3	3.7220	.52132	2.4269	5.0170	3.41	4.32
Total	43	3.6605	.69823	3.4456	3.8754	1.85	5.63

Table 14

ANOVA for PADV-R mean for participants of various occupations

	Sum of Squares	df	Mean Square	F	Sig.
Between Groups	5.146	6	.858	2.014	.089*
Within Groups	15.330	36	.426		
Total	20.476	42			

* The mean difference is significant at the .05 level.

An interesting result occurred when analyzing the individual sections of the PADV-R for participants of various occupations. While the mean PADV-R score was not significantly different for the participants of various occupations, the results of the Analysis of Variance (ANOVA) for Section IV of the PADV-R indicate that there is enough evidence to reject the null hypothesis (p-value = 0.008, Table 15). Therefore, there was a significant difference in the mean score for Section IV of the PADV-R for participants of various occupations. The mean score for section IV of the PADV-R ranged from 2.00 for housewives to 5.62 for clerical workers or salespeople.

Table 15

ANOVA for Section IV mean for participants of various occupations

	Sum of Squares	df	Mean Square	F	Sig.
Between Groups	21.511	6	3.585	3.508	.008*
Within Groups	36.793	36	1.022		
Total	58.304	42			

* The mean difference is significant at the .05 level.

Religion of Participants

There were four options given on the questionnaire for the participants to choose from, Protestant, Catholic, No religion, or other. The mean PADV-R score for Protestant participants was 3.66 with a standard deviation of 0.74, while the mean PADV-R score for Catholic participants was 3.59 with a standard deviation of 0.18 and the mean PADV-R score for participants of other religions was 3.74 with a standard deviation of 0.61 (Table 16). The results of the Analysis of Variance (ANOVA) for various religions indicate that there is not enough evidence to reject the null hypothesis (p-value = 0.97, Table 17). Therefore, there is not a significant difference in the mean PADV-R score for participants that are Protestants,

Catholics, and other religions. There were no responses to the *No religion* category.

The results of the religion portion of this study showed that there were no significant differences among the participants regarding religion or even the lack of a religion. The perceptions and attitudes among African American business leaders regarding partner abuse are just about the same among the various religions, and the mean PADV-R scores for these groups indicate that they *somewhat disagreed* with the statements about what constitutes domestic violence. Therefore, no matter if a person is Protestant or Catholic, his or her beliefs about the behaviors that constitute partner abuse are similar. Once again, proving that further education about domestic violence is very important.

Table 16

Descriptive statistics for PADV-R for participants of various religions

	n	Mean	SD	95% Confidence Interval for Mean		Minimum	Maximum
				Lower Bound	Upper Bound		
Protestant	37	3.6599	.73831	3.4137	3.9061	1.85	5.63
Catholic	3	3.5907	.18253	3.1373	4.0442	3.41	3.78
Other	3	3.7375	.61367	2.2130	5.2619	3.23	4.42
Total	43	3.6605	.69823	3.4456	3.8754	1.85	5.63

Table 17

ANOVA for PADV-R mean for participants of various religions

	Sum of Squares	df	Mean Square	F	Sig.
Between Groups	.032	2	.016	.032	.969
Within Groups	20.444	40	.511		
Total	20.476	42			

Although the study only identified significant differences in the attitudes toward and perceptions of domestic violence among African American business leaders based on income, the results indicate that the majority of the participants did not fully understand what constitutes domestic violence. Furthermore, the results from research question three indicated that there is still a significant amount of domestic violence in the African American and many other communities. The results from this study indicate that domestic violence is a significant problem, and there is a need for further study on domestic violence, partner abuse, as well as intimate partner abuse. There has to be some influencing factors that are enable predators to continue to abuse. The role of the social work community is to get out and find out what those factors are in order to put a stop to domestic violence. Lastly, the results of this study indicate that there is a dire need for additional education regarding behaviors and actions that are considered domestic violence and partner abuse.

CHAPTER 5. SUMMARY, CONCLUSIONS, IMPLICATIONS, AND RECOMMENDATIONS

Summary

The purpose of this study was to evaluate the perceptions of and attitudes toward partner abuse among African American business leaders. The following questions were composed to guide this research:

1. Among African American business leaders, are the perceptions and attitudes toward partner abuse based on the level of income in the home?
2. Among African American business leaders, are the perceptions and attitudes held toward partner abuse significantly dependent on the highest level of education completed?
3. Among African American business leaders, is there evidence that partner abuse had occurred based on their relationship with someone who has been or is still in a domestic violence relationship, as measured by the Perceptions of and Attitude toward Domestic Violence Questionnaire - Revised (Yick, 1997)?
4. Among African American business leaders, is there a relationship between the perceptions of partner abuse and various demographic variables such as marital status, occupation, gender, religion, and age?

Based on the review of literature, the following hypotheses were organized by the researcher:

1. Among African American business leaders, there is a variation in the perceptions of and attitudes toward partner abuse based on the level of income in the home.

2. Among African American business leaders, there is a variation in the perceptions of and attitudes toward partner abuse based on the highest level of education completed.

3. Among African American business leaders, there is evidence that partner abuse had occurred based on their relationship with someone who was or is still in a domestic violence relationship, as measured by the Perceptions of and Attitudes toward

    Domestic Violence Questionnaire – Revised (PADV-R) (Yick, 1997).

4. Among African American business leaders, there is a variation in the perceptions of partner abuse based on various demographic variables such as marital status, occupation, gender, religion, and age.

The population targeted for this study was defined as African American business leaders. The attainable population consisted of 152 African American business leaders (80 males and 72 females) currently holding positions in local businesses within the Panhandle of Florida, which included mainly the Panama City and Pensacola areas. Two African American business directories were utilized to obtain the targeted population.

Data was collected using a two-part instrument: the Perceptions of and Attitudes toward Domestic Violence Questionnaire – Revised (PADV-R) (Yick, 1997). Data was collected during the months of May through July 2006 by mailing the survey instrument to 152 African American business people within the Panhandle of Florida. One survey was returned because the company relocated but there was no forwarding address. This reduced the sample to 151. A total of 43 African American business leaders (28%) responded to the survey. This was considered to be a good response rate. The data collected was used to test hypotheses 1, 2, and 4 listed above with Analysis of Variance (ANOVA) at a statistical significance level, alpha, equal to 0.05.

Conclusions, Implications, and Recommendations

Based on the findings of this study, the following conclusions, implications, and recommendations were drawn:

Observation 1

Among African American business leaders there are varieties in the perceptions and attitudes toward partner abuse based on income level. This conclusion was determined based on the following results of the study: the mean PADV-R score for participants earning less than $25,000 was 2.63 (SD = 0.98), meaning that the participants *agreed*. The mean PADV-R score for participants earning between $25,000 and $50,000 was 3.60 (SD = 0.39) and the mean PADV-R score for participants that earn between $50,000 and $75,000 was 3.43 (SD = 0.41), which means that these participants *agreed somewhat*. In addition, the mean PADV-R score for participants that earn between $75,000 and $100,00 was 4.39 (SD = 0.85) and participants that earn $100,000 or more had a mean PADV-R score of 3.78 (SD = 0.66).

An ANOVA was conducted on the mean scores for the various income levels and the results indicated that there was a significant difference at the significance level of 0.05. Therefore, this research study shows that, among African American business leaders, the perceptions of and attitudes toward domestic violence varies with income level. Those below $25,000 *agreed* that behaviors such as hitting, trying to control one's life, not allowing a partner to make any decisions, pushing one's partner, and more are viewed as domestic violence. While those in the other income categories *agreed somewhat* that the above behaviors constitute domestic violence. The participants in the $75,000 – $99,999 bracket *disagreed somewhat* that those behaviors described in the survey constituted domestic violence.

This conclusion is supported by earlier research, which states "In North America, belonging to a minority ethnic group has been thought to be associated with intimate partner violence, but associations have been largely explained by differences in education and income" (Jewkes, 2002, pg. 1424). However, Jewkes also states that in countries such as South Africa, physical abuse was not linked with the usual indicators, which constitute socioeconomic status, such as male and female occupations or unemployment.

The information gathered in this research is relevant to social work in general. As we follow the data, we find that there is room for future research to determine the role income plays in domestic violence. The implication here is that future research could impact the making of new policies and new laws to assist those involved in any way in a domestic dispute, whether victim or perpetrator. The community would benefit from the findings of this research mainly because of the possibilities that would be presented to help re-educate or simply inform its leaders about the issues that arise from domestic violence especially as they pertain to income levels.

It is the responsibility of the researcher to ensure that the results of this study are publicized to the community involved in the study. The researcher plans to contact as many social service agencies within the African American community to give them the results of this study. The researcher recommends that the leaders come together in an effort to build up the community as much as possible. The leaders include civic as well as religious individuals. The leaders can help to inform the public about the importance of domestic violence.

This recommendation is supported by earlier research. Authors Mattson & Ruiz (2005) state that this area of study is extremely relevant, but little research has been conducted on partner abuse or Intimate Partner Violence (IPV) in the minority community.

> Research on violence must take into account the broad social and cultural context within which women live; however, there has been little research on IPV in minority and disadvantaged families, resulting in a dearth of culturally relevant prevention strategies, interventions, and programs to prevent IPV and successfully assist minority women who suffer abuse, (Mattson & Ruiz, 2005, pp. 523-524).

Observation 2

Among African American business leaders in the Florida Panhandle, the level of education did not influence the perceptions of and attitudes toward domestic violence. This conclusion is based on results to the following: the mean PADV-R score for participants with high school degrees was 3.57 (SD = 1.06), while the mean PADV-R score for participants with junior college degrees was 3.67 (SD = 0.70) and the mean PADV-R score for participants with Bachelor's degrees was 3.87 (SD = 0.70). In addition, the mean PADV-R score for participants with Master's degrees was 3.49 (SD = 0.41) and participants with Doctoral degrees had a mean PADV-R score of 3.71 (SD = 0.12). Lastly, an ANOVA was conducted on the mean scores for the various education levels and the results indicated that there was no significant difference at the significance level of 0.05. Therefore, there is not a significant difference in the mean PADVR score for participants of various education levels. So, from this study, it was concluded that the level of education did not influence the perceptions of and attitudes toward domestic violence for African American business leaders.

The researcher hypothesized that education would play a significant role in the perceptions and attitudes of African American business leaders toward partner abuse. However, according to the results, even if one did not complete high school or at the other end of the spectrum, one has received a doctoral degree, it is not necessarily relevant to one's thoughts about partner abuse. These results are relevant because they show that formal education is not one of the factors that contribute to domestic violence. This conclusion is supported by earlier research, which states:

> High levels of female empowerment seem to be protective against intimate partner violence, but power can be derived from many sources such as education, income, and community roles and not all of these convey equal protection or do so in a direct manner. In many studies, high educational attainment of women was associated with low levels of violence. The same find has been noted for men. Education confers social empowerment via social networks, self-confidence, and an ability to use information and resources available in society, and may also translate into wealth. The relation between intimate partner violence and female education, however, is complex. In the USA and South Africa the relation has an inverted U-shape with protection at the lowest and highest educational levels (Jewkes, 2002, pg. 1425).

The researcher recommends that further research should be completed to determine the following questions. What would have an impact on the attitudes and perceptions? Will informal education do it? Will trainings and seminars affect the business-minded men and women of the Panhandle of Florida? While increased awareness may be needed within African American churches, schools, and communities; the question is raised, how would they get the awareness? Another community having similar problems with domestic violence has been identified. In an article written by Susan Grossman (2005), she discusses the writer Carol Kaufman (2003) who has researched the Jewish community and has written a book entitled *Sins of Omission: The Jewish Community's Reaction to Domestic Violence*. Both communities lack the wherewithal to enlighten their members on the seriousness of domestic violence. Grossman (2005) states that:

> The result of her work is a comprehensive overview of the community's beliefs, interventions (or lack thereof), reactions, and misperceptions of the problem of spousal abuse. Kaufman carefully documents how denial about the existence of abuse, as well as the lack of knowledge or misinformation about the best way to intervene, prevents many rabbis from responding to the issue (p. 22).

Are there organizations within either community that will step up and take on the challenge of helping increase the awareness of their people in order to help stop domestic violence? If so, what organizations will do it? The implication for increased awareness is that there are organizations such as the Chamber of Commerce, the United Way, fraternal groups or sororities that are usually willing to help any community. Also within the African American community, there are organizations such as the National Association for the Advancement of Colored People (NAACP) and ministerial alliances. These groups have great voices within their and other communities. These groups also have the ability to help change or implement policies that will help the victims of domestic violence.

Observation 3

Among African American business leaders, many know of a family member or friend who has experienced physical or verbal abuse. This conclusion is based on results to the following: the participants were asked whether or not a family member or friend had confided in him or her about partner abuse that he or she had experienced or is still experiencing. Of the 43 participants, 39 of them responded *yes* to at least one question in Section V of the PADV-R survey, which indicated that they had been told or known of any African American friends or family members who have experienced physical or verbal abuse. Of the 39 participants that responded *yes* to at least one of the Section V questions, 13 of them responded *yes* to all six questions in the section, 8 of them responded *yes* to five of the six questions, 4 of them responded *yes* to four of the six questions, 4 of them responded *yes* to three of the six questions, 4 of them responded *yes* to two of the six questions, and 6 of them responded *yes* to one of the six questions. These results indicate that almost everyone who completed a questionnaire was told or knew of an African American friend or family member who had experienced physical or verbal abuse.

The conclusion is consistent with research completed by Yoshioka, Gilbert, El-Bassel, & Baig-Amin (2003). These researchers conducted a study among Asian, African American, and Hispanic women. This study discussed the implications of disclosure to friends or family members about their domestic violence issues. According to this study, Yoshioka and colleagues (2003) discovered that African American women did not disclose as much as did the Hispanic women or the South Asian women. They recognized by the responses from the participants that African American women more than likely blamed themselves for the abuse that was imposed on them based on the discrimination that African American men received for so many years. Because of the blame, many of the women were determined to keep their abuse to themselves. If the women did tell anyone about the abuse, that was all they did, they chose not to press charges against the men mainly because it would cause them more suffering. The majority of the participants of the study completed in the Panhandle of Florida indicated that they knew friends or family members who had been abused or is still in the abusive relationship. This information was obtained based on Section V of the PADV-R survey.

The researcher recommends that the community leaders formulate counseling programs in areas where the members of the community will be able to have reasonably easy access to counseling if they choose to utilize the services. The implication is that within the community this may be helpful for victims as well as friends or family in coming forward with information about domestic violence. This may also help the social service agencies to provide more services or to reorganize the current structures to better serve the public.

Observation 4

Among African American business leaders, there was not a significant difference between males and females in their attitudes and perceptions regarding partner abuse. This conclusion is based on results to the following: the participants were asked to indicate their gender. Of the 43 participants 20 (46.5%) were men and 23 (53.5%) were women. The mean PADV-R score for male participants was 3.63 ($\underline{SD}$ = 0.56), while the mean PADV-R score for female participants was 3.69 ($\underline{SD}$ = 0.81). In addition, an ANOVA was conducted on the means scores by gender and the results indicated that there was not a significant difference at the significance level of 0.05.

Research on domestic violence or intimate partner violence has not proven without a doubt the exact causes of why perpetrators pounce on victims. However, there are risk factors, which are linked to domestic violence. One researcher who states that a gender norm is a risk factor debates the above conclusion. "Furthermore, measurement of social conditions thought to be risk factors, such as the status of women, gender norms, and socioeconomic status poses difficulties, especially across cultures" (Jewkes, 2002, p. 1423).

The implication here is that even though this current study states that there is no significant difference between male and female attitudes and perceptions about partner abuse in the Panhandle of Florida, it may exist elsewhere. This leaves the door open for further research to determine just how different males and females are when it comes to their thought and attitudes towards domestic violence.

Observation 5

Among African American business leaders, there was not a significant difference in the attitude and perception regarding partner abuse between the two age groups, those below 50 and those above 50. This conclusion is based on the following results: the mean PADV-R score for participants less than 50 years of age was 3.72 ($\underline{SD}$ = 0.86), while the mean PADV-R score for participants 50 and over was 3.62 ($\underline{SD}$ = 0.59). In addition, an ANOVA was conducted on the means scores by age group and the results indicated that there was not a significant difference at the significance level of 0.05.

This conclusion is supported by earlier research. "Age, for example, has occasionally been noted to be a risk factor for such violence with a greater risk attached to youth, but in most research a relation with age of either partner has not been seen" (Jewkes, 2002), p. 1423). The implication for future studies is vast. The possibilities for research to be conducted on men and women of all ages are endless. The research may help to determine what triggers domestic violence behavior among all ages.

Observation 6

Among African American business leaders, there was not a significant difference for married and unmarried participants regarding the attitude and perception of partner abuse. This conclusion is based on the following results: the mean PADV-R score for married participants was 3.62 ($\underline{SD}$ = 0.64), while the mean PADV-R score for unmarried participants was 3.74 ($\underline{SD}$ = 0.82). In addition, an ANOVA was conducted on the means scores by marital status and the results indicated that there was not a significant difference at the significance level of 0.05.

Observation 7

Among African American business leaders, there was a significant difference for participants of various occupations regarding the attitude and perception of partner abuse. This conclusion is based on the following results: The mean PADV-R score for unemployed participants was 3.56 ($\underline{SD}$ = 0.31), while the mean PADV-R score for self-employed participants was 3.72 ($\underline{SD}$ = 0.52) and the mean PADV-R score for participants that are clerical workers or salespeople was 3.98 ($\underline{SD}$ = 0.94). In addition, the mean PADV-R score for participants that are semi-professionals or managers was 3.48 ($\underline{SD}$ = 0.52) and participants that are professionals had a mean PADV-R score of 3.85 ($\underline{SD}$ = 0.67). In addition, an ANOVA was conducted on the means scores by occupation and the results indicated that there was a significant difference at the significance level of 0.05.

An interesting result occurred when analyzing the individual sections of the PADV-R for participants of various occupations. While the mean PADV-R score was not significantly different for the participants of various occupations, the results of the Analysis of Variance (ANOVA) for Section IV of the PADV-R indicate that there is enough evidence to reject the null hypothesis (p-value = 0.008). Therefore, there was a significant difference in the mean score for Section IV of the PADV-R for participants of various occupations. The mean score for section IV of the PADV-R ranged from 2.00 for housewives to 5.62 for clerical workers or salespeople.

Observation 8

Among African American business leaders, there was no significant difference regarding the perception and attitudes regarding partner abuse, when it came to religion or even the lack of a religion. This conclusion is based on the following results: There were four options given on the questionnaire for the participants to choose from, Protestant, Catholic, No religion, or other. The mean PADV-R score for Protestant participants was 3.66 ($\underline{SD}$ = 0.74), while the mean PADV-R score for Catholic participants was 3.59 ($\underline{SD}$ = 0.18) and the mean PADV-R score for participants of other religions was 3.74 ($\underline{SD}$ = 0.61).). In addition, an ANOVA was conducted on the means scores by gender and the results indicated that there was not a significant difference at the significance level of 0.05.

There are implications for future research. One result of this research is that formal education, such as obtaining a bachelor, masters, or doctoral degree, did not make a significant difference in the attitudes and perceptions of the African American businessman or businesswoman towards partner abuse. According to the results of the level of education and its correlation to domestic violence, it was determined that the level of education did not determine the attitudes and perceptions of partner abuse among African American business leaders. The results showed that the participants with a high school degree and those with a junior college degree were very close in their thoughts and perceptions of domestic violence. The study also revealed that those participants with higher degrees such a bachelor, masters, doctorate, or professional (MD or JD), were only a few points apart in their mean scores. Therefore, the results showed no significant difference in the mean PADV-R score for the participants based on their different educational levels. The implication of this study regarding education is that formal education is not a good indicator of attitudes and perceptions of partner abuse among African American business leaders. However, it could indicate that informal education or awareness about is domestic violence is necessary in the African American communities.

A recommendation for community change would be that the social service or social work arena makes itself known to the community members in a more tangible way. One way would be to hold one or more health fairs or health seminars in order to inform the community of what is available to them via the many social service agencies in the area. The implication is that the community becomes more aware of availability as well as the locations of the various agencies that offer many different services to African American business leaders. This may not only assist with education and awareness for domestic violence or intimate partner abuse, but also a host of other issues and problems that impact the African American community in the Panhandle of Florida.

Implications for Social Work

Many thoughts and ideas permeate our society about stopping domestic violence. However, we have yet to come up with a solution that has proven to annihilate domestic violence. The implications for social work include finding ways of understanding the problems of partner abuse within the African American community as it relates to research, education, policy and law, and social work practice.

Research

One way to attempt to stop domestic violence is the continuation of research within the social work arena. Research might actually help society to see what's actually behind the closed doors. The result of this study has implications for research. These results show that only a small percentage of the Panhandle of Florida may respond to mail surveys. This could indicate that other methodologies may work better to get the necessary results regarding the attitudes and perceptions of partner abuse among African American business leaders. Face-to-Face interviews might yield a higher response and more information could be obtained from follow-up questions, than can be obtained through closed ended questions, especially those on a mailed survey. However, the research needs to continue in order to make that determination.

One of the limitations of this study is the questionnaire design. In retrospect the researcher could have structured the questions differently for better responses. One area would be the need for further disclosure of domestic violence by family members or friends. This methodology utilized forced choice of either a yes or a no, which did not provide a clear understanding of the nature of the abuse. A preferred methodology would have utilized follow up questions, and obtained more information on the nature of abuse.

Another limitation of this study was the utilization of survey instead of interviews or focused groups. This limitation was based on the way the surveys were completed for this mailed survey. Surveys were returned with one answer circled, and then crossed out, and the next answer given was at the other end of the spectrum. From these responses, it appeared that the questions were not very clear to the participants. For practical purposes, as well as to get the most out of a subject matter of this magnitude, it would be more effective to conduct face-to-face interviews.

Education

As stated earlier, formal education is not a significant factor in the attitudes and perceptions of partner abuse among African American business leaders. This, does not however, mean that education cannot play a definite role in enhancing the community's awareness to partner abuse. The social work school system could be very successful in its assistance in educating the community via educating its students in order for them to better serve the community. Eva Nowakowski (2006) referenced Cohn et al, (2002) when she stated:

> Schools of social work recognize the complexity and importance of family violence education. Family violence content, by way of elective courses, is encouraged by the Council on Social Work Education (CSWE) (2004), yet CSWE has no specific requirements mandating that the issue of family violence be discussed on any level. There is an expectation that a social work program educating

students for practice must at some point address the problem of family violence (pgs. 89-90).

Policy and Law

The National Association of Social Workers is an organization that has made great strides in the government and in society in general by lobbying for certain policy and laws to be passed. Social workers are great policy makers. In order for domestic violence or partner abuse to be halted, policies and laws need to be enacted to help protect the victims, appropriately punish the perpetrators and to enlighten the community about the crime of domestic violence in order to prevent the crime from continuing. The following bills have been passed and supported by the National Association of Social Workers. They are working tirelessly on a variety of issues. Domestic violence may be next on a future agenda. Thanks to an ambitious 100-hour agenda by the new House Speaker Nancy Pelosi (CA-8), the U.S. House of Representatives has passed a number of bills in the first two weeks of Congress. A number of these bills are of interest to social workers.

1. The House passed H.R. 5, College Student Relief Act of 2007, on January 17 by a vote of 356-71. H.R. 5 would decrease interest on federal student loans in half over 5 years. The bill now heads to the Senate, where Sen. Kennedy (MA) chairman of the Health, Education, Labor and Pensions Committee, is cosponsoring a significantly broader rate cut bill S. 282, College Student Relief Act of 2007, that is expected go through his panel first. The Senate bill, in addition to halving the interest rate, also would cap loan repayments at 15 percent of income and increase the maximum Pell grant from $4,050 to $5,100. Kennedy aides said his committee will mark up college affordability legislation in February, though it won't necessarily be the bill he cosponsored.

2. The House passed H.R. 2, the Fair Minimum Wage Act of 2007, on January 10 by a vote of 315-116. H.R. 2 would increase the federal minimum wage from $5.15/hour to $7.25/hour over two years. The Senate is expected to take up the bill during the week of January 22. Senator Baucus (MT) wants to include small business tax breaks in the Senate version of the bill. Other members are working to include amendments to the bill. National Association of Social Workers is supporting the passage of a clean bill, with no amendments.

3. Sen. Inouye (HI) has introduced a number of bills related to social workers; National Center for Social Work Research Act of 2007, S. 106 to establish a center for social work research in the federal government; Strengthen Social Work Training Act of 2007, S. 64 to make sure social workers are eligible for federal grant programs related to health care training such as the National Health Service Corps.

4. Rep. Towns (NY-10) introduced H.R. 425, a bill to authorize the use of clinical social workers to conduct evaluations to determine work-related emotional and mental illnesses.

5. Additionally, we are expecting bills to be introduced on Medicare Part B payments affecting social workers, small business insurance reform and behavioral health coverage, mental health parity, medical records privacy, restoration of Medicaid funding cuts and SCHIP expansion (National Association of Social Workers online, 2007).

Social Work Practice

Social work practice is important aspect in all communities. Social workers sometimes work in areas where they are known as case managers; they help manage the cases presented to their agency. The problem sometimes is that, especially in the case of domestic violence, people do not report their problems until they are in serious trouble. At which point, it becomes necessary for the case manager to act swiftly to assess the situation and try to provide services as soon as possible for the client. The implications for practice is that if there is no research, no education, and no new policies, or laws, the practice of social work becomes limited because services are not provided as needed.

> Case managers must also help consumers understand that assessment is conducted to determine service referral and benefits entitlements and is not an automatic guarantee of services or program acceptance. Because people often delay seeking help until they are in crisis, being able to successfully explore client expectations, to engage clients or caregivers, and to coherently interpret the program's agenda are important front-end issues. Staff should be able to discuss their program's philosophy and any policies, procedures, or other restrictions that may interfere with the worker's ability to follow through (Raiff & Shore, 1993, pp. 28-32).

Social workers play an active role in society. This study shows that there is still much work to be done in the area of research with regards to domestic violence, partner abuse, or intimate partner violence.

REFERENCES

Ahn, B. (2002). *The perceptions of and attitudes toward partner abuse among first generation Korean-Americans: Their relationships to the incidence of partner abuse.* Unpublished doctoral dissertation, Louisiana State University and A&M College, Baton Rouge.

Bandura, A., Ross, D., & Ross, S. A. (1961). Transmission of aggression through imitation of aggressive models. *Journal of Abnormal and Social Psychology, 67,* 575-582.

Bent-Goodley, T. B. (2004). Perceptions of domestic violence: A dialogue with African American women. *Health & Social Work,* 29(4), 307-347.

Berlinger, J. S. (2004). *The Journal of Nursing, 34,* 42-47.

Berry, D.B. (2000). *The domestic violence sourcebook.* Chicago, IL: Lowell House

Billingsley, A. (1968). *Black families in White America.* Englewood Cliffs: Prentice Hall.

Blackwell, J. (1985). *The Black community: Diversity and unity (2ⁿᵈ ed.).* New York: Harper & Row.

Brannon, N. (1983). Marriage and family therapy with Black clients: Methods and structure. In C. Obudho (Ed.), *Black marriage and family therapy* (pp. 169-188). Westport, CT: Greenwood.

Caetano, R.; Schafer, J., & Cunradi, C.B. (2001). Alcohol-related intimate partner violence among White, Black, and Hispanic couples in the United States. *Alcohol Research & Health, 25, 58-65.*

Caracci, G. (2003). Violence against women: Mental health and the United Nations. *International Journal of Mental Health, 32,* 36-53.

Cha-Jua, S.K. (2001). Slavery, racist violence, American apartheid: The case for reparations. *New Politics, 8.* Retrieved on September 13, 2005, from http://www.wpunj.edu/~newpol/isse32/chajua31.htm

Cohn, F., Salmon, M., & Stobo, J. (2002). Report: *Confronting chronic neglect: The education and training of health professionals on family violence.* Committee on the Training Needs of Health Professionals to Respond to Family Violence Board on Children, Youth, and Families. Washington, DC, National Academy Press.

Crenshaw, K. (1994). *Mapping the margins: Intersectionality, identity-politics, and violence against women of color.* In M.A. Fireman & R. Mykitiuk (Eds.). The public nature of private violence: The discovery of domestic abuse (pp. 93-117). New York: Routledge.

Dakis, L. (1995). Dade County's domestic violence plan: An integrated approach. *Trial, 31,* 44.

Ellsberg, M., & Heise, L. (2002). Bearing witness: Ethics in domestic violence research. *The Lancet, 359,* 1599-1604.

Employment discrimination & Title VII of the Civil Rights Act of 1964. *Harvard Law Review (1971), 84,* p. 1109-1317.

Eng, P. (1995). *Domestic violence in Asian/Pacific island communities.* In D.L. Adams (Ed.), Health issues for women of color: A cultural diversity perspective (pp. 78-88). Thousand Oaks, CA: Sage.

Evans, N. (2005). Domestic violence: Recognizing the signs. *Pediatric Nursing, 17,* p. 14-16.

Feagin, J., & Sikes, M. (1994). *Living with racism.* Boston, MA: Beacon.

Felson, R. B., Messner, S. F., Hoskin, A. W., & Deane, G. (2002). Reasons for reporting and not reporting domestic violence to the police. *Criminology, 40,* 617-636.

Gamache, D. (1998). Domination and control: The social context of dating violence. In B. Levy (Ed.), *Dating violence: Young women in danger,* 2nd ed., (pp. 69-83). Seattle, WA: Seal Press.

Gelles, R.J., & Cornell, C.P. (1990). *Intimate violence in families.* Newbury Park, CA: Sage.

Grown, C., Gupta, G. R. & Pande, R. (2005). Taking action to improve women's health through gender equality and women's empowerment. *Lancet, 365,* p. 541-544.

Greenblat, C. S. (1985). "Don't hit your wife...unless...": Preliminary findings on normative support for the use of physical force by husbands. *Victimology, 10,* p. 221-241.

Grossman, S. (2005). *Sins of omission: The Jewish community's reaction to domestic violence, by Carol G. Kaufman.* Retrieved on 12/3/2006 from: http://proquest.umi.com.

Ho, C.K. (1990). Analysis of domestic violence in Asian American communities: A multicultural approach to counseling. In L.S. Brown & M. Root (Eds.) *Diversity and complexity in feminist therapy* (pp. 129-150). New York: Harrington Park.

Intimate Partner Violence. (2003). Department of Health & Human Services, Centers for Disease Control & Prevention, National Center for Injury Prevention & Control.

Jamison, W. (1999). Confidentiality in social research. Retrieved on November 23, 2003 from: http://www.wpi.edu/Academics/Projects/confidentiality.html

Jewell, K.S. (1988). *Survival of the Black family*. New York, NY: Praeger.

Jewkes, R. (2002). Intimate partner violence: Causes and prevention. *The Lancet, 359*, 1423-1429.

Kaufman, C. G. (2003). *Sins of omission: The Jewish community's reaction to domestic violence*. Boulder, CO: Westview Publishing.

Keith, V. M., & Norwood, R. S. (1997). Marital strain and depressive symptoms among African Americans. Retrieved on August 1, 2005, from

http://www.public_html/prba/persp/spring1997/vkeith.html

Langford, D.R. (2000). Pearls, pith, and provocation: Developing a safety protocol in qualitative research involving battered women. *Qualitative Health Research, 10*(1), 133- 142.

Lee, R. K.; Thompson, V. L. S.; & Mechanic, M. B. (2002). Intimate partner violence and women of color: A call for innovations. *American Journal of Public Health, 92*, 530-534.

Leedy, P., and Ormrod, J. (2016). *Practical research: Planning and design* (11th ed.). Boston, MA: Pearson.

Lown, E. A, & Vega, W. A. (2001). Prevalence and predicators of physical partner abuse among Mexican American women. *American Journal of Public Health, 91*, 441-445.

Lutenbacher, M., Cohen, A., & Mitzel, J. (2003). Do we really help? Perspectives of abused women. *Journal of Public Health Nursing, 20*, 56-64.

McCollum, V. J. C. (1997). The evolution of the African American family personality: Considerations for family therapy. *Journal of Multicultural Counseling & Development, 25*, p. 219-230.

Malley-Morrison, K. & Hines, D. A. (2004). *Family violence in a cultural perspective: Defining, understanding, and combating abuse.* Thousand Oaks, CA: Sage.

Mattson, S. & Ruiz, E. (2005). Intimate partner violence in the Latino community and its effect on children. *Health Care for Women International, 26*, pp. 523-529.

Merriam-Webster Online Dictionary. Retrieved on December 20, 2005 from http://www.m-w.com/

Miller, C. E., & Mullins, B. K. (2002). Lifelong learning to reduce domestic violence. *International Journal of Lifelong Education, 21*, 474-484.

Muro-Ruiz, D. (2002). State of the art: The logic of violence. *Politics, 22*, 109-117.

National Association of Social Workers Online. Retrieved on January 30, 2007 from   http://www.socialworkers.org/advocacy/updates/2007/012307.asp

Nowakowski, E. (2006). *An analysis of family violence, dating violence perpetration and social learning theory.* Unpublished doctoral dissertation, Barry University School of Social Work, Miami.

Nunnaly, J. (1978). *Psychometric theory.* New York, NY: McGraw-Hill.

Oetzel, J. & Duran, B. (2004). Intimate partner violence in American Indian and/or Alaska native communities: A social ecological framework of determinants and interventions. American Indian

& Alaska Native Mental Health Research: *The Journal of the National Center, 11*, 49-69.

Parker, B. & Ulrich, Y. (1990). A protocol of safety: Research on abuse of women. *Journal of Nursing Research, 39*, 248-250.

Program for multicultural health: Cultural competency. Retrieved on October 10, 2005 from   http://www.med.umich.edu/multicultural/ccp/cdv.htm

Raiff, N. R. & Shore, B. K. (1993). *Advanced case management: New strategies for the nineties.* Newbury, CA: Sage Publications, Inc.

Ramos, B.M., Carlson, B.E., & McNutt, L. (2004). Lifetime abuse, mental health, and African American women. *Journal of Family Violence, 19*, p. 153-164.

Rankin, B. H. & Falk, W. W. (1991). Race, region, & earnings: Blacks & Whites in the South. *Rural Sociology, 56*, 224-237.

Robin, R. W., Chester, B., & Rasmussen, J. K. (1998). Intimate violence in a southwestern American Indian tribal community. *Cultural Diversity and Mental Health, 4*, 335-344.

Robinson, G. E. (2003). Violence against women in North America. *Archives of Women's Mental Health, 6*, 185-191.

Rossman, M. H. (1995). *Negotiating graduate school: A guide for graduate students.* Thousand Oaks, CA: Sage Publications.

Schulz, A.; Israel, B.; Williams, D.; Parker, E.; Becker, A.; & James, S. (2000). *Journal of Social Science Medicine, 51*, 1639-1653.

Slack, T. & Jensen, L. (2002). Race, ethnicity, and underemployment in non-metropolitan America: A 30-year profile. *Rural Sociology, 67*, p. 208-233.

Straus, M.A., Gelles, R.J., & Steinmetz, S. (1980). *Behind closed doors: Violence in the American family.* Garden City, NJ: Anchor.

Uniform Crime Reports, 2004. Retrieved on July 28, 2005, from: http//www.fbi.gov/ucr/ucr.htm

West, C.M. (1998). Lifting the "political gag order": Breaking the silence around partner violence in ethnic minority families. In J.L. Jasinski & L.M. Williams (Eds.), *Partner violence: A comprehensive review of 20 years of research* (pp. 184-209). Thousand Oaks: Sage.

Wilson, L., & Stith, S. (1991). Culturally sensitive therapy with Black clients. *Journal of Multicultural Counseling and Development, 19,* 32-42.

Yick, A.G. (In Press). Role of culture and context: Ethical issues in research with Asian Americans and immigrants in intimate violence. *Journal of Family Violence.*

Yick, A.G. (1997). *Chinese-American's perceptions of and experiences with domestic violence and factors related to their psychological well-being.* Unpublished doctoral dissertation. University of California, Los Angeles.

Yoshioka, M. R., Gilbert, L., El-Bassel, N., & Baig-Amin, M. (2003). Social support and disclosure of abuse: Comparing South Asian, African American, and Hispanic battered women. *Journal of Family Violence, 18,* pp. 171-180.

APPENDIX A. QUESTIONNAIRE

Perceptions of and Attitudes toward
Domestic Violence Questionnaire

I. We are interested in your opinions about what behaviors are considered violence between spouses or couples. Please read the key sentence with various behaviors listed below from a to n, inserted in the blank of the key sentence. Answer how much you agree or disagree whether the behavior is considered violence between spouses or couples. There are six choices for you to choose from. Circle the number that best reflects your opinion.

1 = STRONGLY AGREE	4 = DISAGREE SOMEWHAT
2 = AGREE	5 = DISAGREE
3 = AGREE SOMEWHAT	6 = STRONGLY DISAGREE

Key Sentence:
(_____) is considered violence between spouses or couples.
(INSERT WITH ITEMS BELOW)

a. Punching one's spouse/ partner's face real hard during an argument....1...2...3...4...5...6

b. Arguing with one's spouse/partner ....1...2...3...4...5...6

c. Forcing one's spouse/partner to have sex ....1...2...3...4...5...6

d. Constantly threatening to use a butcher knife to hurt one's spouse/partner ....1...2...3...4...5...6

e. Demanding to know where one's spouse/partner is all the time ....1...2...3...4...5...6

f. Disagreeing with one's spouse/partner about how much to spend on personal items ....1...2...3...4...5...6

g. Criticizing one's spouse/partner in front of others ....1...2...3...4...5...6

h. Throwing objects like an ash tray at one's spouse/partner ....1...2...3...4...5...6

i. Pushing one's spouse/partner ....1...2...3...4...5...6

j. Not allowing spouse/ partner to make any decisions ....1...2...3...4...5...6

k. Disagreeing about who will do certain household chores....1...2...3...4...5...6

l. Always disregarding one's spouse's/partner's opinions and feelings ....1...2...3...4...5...6

m. Not being aware of one's spouse's/partner's feelings on a political issue ....1...2...3...4...5...6

n. Not allowing one's spouse/partner to have a bank account in his/her name ....1...2...3...4...5...6

II.   People have different opinions about how to handle family matters and how to solve problems in the family. Please read the key sentence with various possible causes of violence listed below from a to j, inserted in the blank of the sentence. Answer how much you agree or disagree. Again, you will choose your answer from six choices.

1 = STRONGLY AGREE	4 = DISAGREE SOMEWHAT
2 = AGREE	5 = DISAGREE
3 = AGREE SOMEWHAT	6 = STRONGLY DISAGREE

a.   In general, it is okay for a man to hit his wife/partner ....1...2...3...4...5...6

b.   Spanking a child is an effective way to discipline ....1...2...3...4...5...6

c.   It is important to have a family meeting at least once a month to discuss any family problems ....1...2...3...4...5...6

d.   Hitting is a good way to solve problems ....1...2...3...4...5...6

e.   It is important for a husband and a wife to resolve conflicts before going to bed ....1...2...3...4...5...6

f.   Hitting should be used if nothing else works ....1...2...3...4...5...6

g.   Hitting a child with a belt is an appropriate form of discipline ....1...2...3...4...5...6

h.   In general, it is okay for a woman to hit her husband/partner ....1...2...3...4...5...6

i.   Communication is the most important thing in a marriage ....1...2...3...4...5...6

j.   The use of physical punishment teaches children self-control ....1...2...3...4...5...6

III. People have different opinions about why violence happens between spouses or couples. We are interested in your opinions about what might cause violence between spouses or couples. Please read the key sentence with various possible causes of violence listed below from a to o, inserted in the blank of the sentence. Answer how much you agree or disagree. Again, you will choose your answer form six choices.

1 = STRONGLY AGREE	4 = DISAGREE SOMEWHAT
2 = AGREE	5 = DISAGREE
3 = AGREE SOMEWHAT	6 = STRONGLY DISAGREE

Key Sentence:

(_____) causes a man to use violence on his wife/partner.
(INSERT ITEMS BELOW)

a. Job pressure ....1...2...3...4...5...6

b. An overcrowded house....1...2...3...4...5...6

c. Inability to control a bad temper ....1...2...3...4...5...6

d. A woman wanting to make more decisions in the home ....1...2...3...4...5...6

e. Past experiences with violence during childhood ....1...2...3...4...5...6

f. Lack of education ....1...2...3...4...5...6

g. Arguments that get out of hand ....1...2...3...4...5...6

h. Beliefs that women are the properties of men ....1...2...3...4...5...6

i. Mental illness ....1...2...3...4...5...6

j. Belief that men are authority figures over
    women ....1...2...3...4...5...6

k. Lack of trust in a marriage ....1...2...3...4...5...6

l. Poverty ....1...2...3...4...5...6

m. Alcohol ....1...2...3...4...5...6

n. Belief that wives should be obedient ....1...2...3...4...5...6

o. Drugs ....1...2...3...4...5...6

IV. Pecople have different opinions about when it is or isn't acceptable to hit.

Read the key sentence with various situations listed below from a to k, inserted in the blank of the sentence. Answer how much you agree or disagree. You will have to choose your answer from six choices.

1 = STRONGLY AGREE	4 = DISAGREE SOMEWHAT
2 = AGREE	5 = DISAGREE
3 = AGREE SOMEWHAT	6 = STRONGLY DISAGREE

Key Sentence:
You just found out that a man hit his wife real hard because _____.
(INSERT ITEMS BELOW)

a. he caught her having an affair ....1...2...3...4...5...6

b. he found her drunk ....1...2...3...4...5...6

c. he acted in self-defense ....1...2...3...4...5...6

d. she was screaming hysterically ....1...2...3...4...5...6

e. she was unwilling to have sex....1...2...3...4...5...6

f. she was always nagging ....1...2...3...4...5...6

g. he was in a bad mood ....1...2...3...4..5...6

h. she was trying to hurt their child ....1...2...3...4...5...6

i. does not spend enough time at home ....1...2...3...4...5...6

j. he found her flirting with someone else ....1...2...3...4...5...6

k. she did not obey him ....1...2...3...4...5...6

V. Have you ever been told or know of any African American friends or family members who have experienced following situations? Please answer yes or no. If your answer is yes, circle 1, and if your answer is no, circle 2.

		Yes	No
a.	Been pushed or grabbed by their spouse/partner?	1	2
b.	Been threatened with a gun or knife by their spouse/partner?	1	2
c.	Been verbally insulted by their spouse/partner?	1	2
d.	Been forced to have sex by their spouse/partner?	1	2
e.	Been slapped by their spouse/partner?	1	2
f.	Not been allowed to leave the house because their spouse/partner would not allow it	1	2

Participant Profile Form

VI. Now I want to ask you some questions about yourself. Again, all answers will be confidential.

1. Gender.
    Male 1
    Female 2

2. How old are you? _____

3. Are you currently married, living with someone, widowed, divorced, separated, or never married?

    Married 1
    Living with someone 2
    Widowed 3
    Divorced.. 4
    Separated 5
    Never married 6

4. What is your occupation?

    Unemployed 1
    Housewife 2
    Student 3
    Manual work 4
    Skilled work 5
    Clerical, salesperson 6
    Semi-professional, manager 7
    Professional.. 8
    Self-employed.. 9

5. What is the household's total annual income? $_____

6. What is the highest degree or diplomas you have attained? (Circle the highest degree)

Less than high school 1
High school diploma (or equivalent) 2
Junior college degree (A.A.) 3
Bachelor's degree (B.A., B.S.) 4
Master's degree (M.A., M.S.) 5
Doctorate (Ph.D.) 6
Professional (M.D., J.D., etc.) 7

7. What is your religion?

Protestant 1
Catholic 2
No religion 3
Other 4
If other, please specify_____

APPENDIX B. INFORMATION ABOUT RESEARCH PARTICIPANTS' RIGHTS

Study Title: "Perceptions and Attitudes of Partner Abuse among African Americans"

Performance Site: School of Human Services, Capella University

Researchers: The following researchers are available for questions about this study, M-F, 8:00a.m. – 5:00p.m. Ann-Marie Jones, MSW, LGSW, 555-xxx-xxxx

Purpose of the Study: The purpose of this research project is to evaluate the perceptions and attitudes that African American business leaders have about domestic violence.

Participants: African American business leaders, 18 years old and older, living in the Emerald Coast Region of Florida: Panama City, Destin, Fort Walton Beach, and Pensacola.

Study Procedures: Participants will spend approximately 20 minutes completing a questionnaire, which was mailed to participants' business address. Participants will be asked to give opinions about definitions of domestic violence, what causes domestic violence, level of education completed, as well as level of income.

Selection of Participants: Participants will be selected from two business directories utilized in the Panhandle of Florida. The Emerald Coast Black Pages (2001-2002) and Harambee, The Black Business Directory of the Greater Pensacola Area.

Benefits: The information collected will assist service providers and policy-makers in understanding perceptions and attitudes of domestic violence in the African American community so that they can help this community more effectively.

Risks: The survey may ask some sensitive questions that may or may not make participants feel uncomfortable. To minimize risk, it is recommended that participants do not discuss answers with spouse or significant other. There may also be a risk of participants experiencing negative thoughts and feelings when completing this questionnaire; this is not the intent of the researcher. A list of domestic violence organizations have been provided in the event someone has any questions about domestic violence.

Voluntary Participation: Participation in the study is strictly voluntary. Participants may choose to return or not to return the questionnaire, or choose not to answer any particular questions without any consequences.

Privacy: All information collected will remain confidential and private. The questionnaire will have an identification number for mailing purposes only. The original list with names will only be referenced for non-response follow-up mailings. Participants' name will be checked off the mailing list when questionnaire is returned. Participants' name will never be placed on the questionnaire, nor will their responses ever be associated with their names. In addition, after all non-response follow-up procedures are completed, the original list, including individual names will be destroyed. Therefore, after this point, no potential connection between responses and individual names will exist. Participant is aware that by answering the questions and returning the survey, the participant is providing and documenting his/her consent.

Summary of Findings: If you are interested, you could receive a summary of the findings of this research. You can feel free to request this in writing. Please be aware that your name and address would be needed if this is something you choose to request. This is not required in order to complete the survey.

Confidentiality: All information obtained from the surveys will be kept in strict confidence and only the researcher will have the information. The information will be kept in a locked safe until such time as it is shredded.

Compensation: Completion of this questionnaire is strictly on a voluntary basis. A Limited Edition, Brilliantly Uncirculated Florida State Quarter is given as appreciation for the completion of this Questionnaire. You will also have the knowledge that you are helping future service providers to understand more about domestic violence.

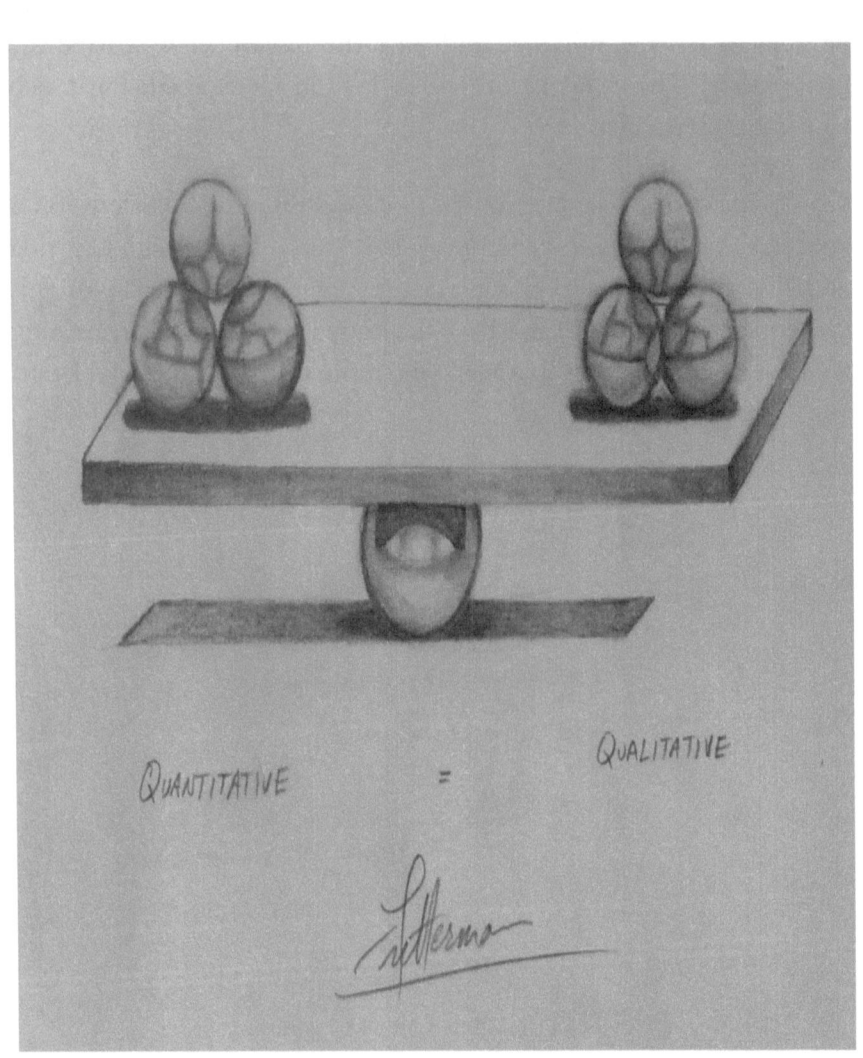

QUANTITATIVE = QUALITATIVE